"How can we become the kind of Christ-followers whose faith is contagious, whose lives make others thirsty for God, who know in our own hearts that our faith is working? Tod Bolsinger addresses these crucial questions with biblical integrity, personal insight, real-life examples, and an easy-to-grasp style. Read *Show Time*. You will see how Christ can show through you in a 'show me' world!"

Leighton Ford, president, Leighton Ford Ministries

"This is a wise and very worthwhile book. It offers us an inspiring progression of spiritual guidance to an authentic practice of our faith."

Max De Pree, chairman emeritus, Herman Miller, Inc.

"*Show Time* gets down to business! Though Tod Bolsinger is a careful biblical scholar and a Ph.D. theologian, he writes for real people who yearn to live out their faith in the real world each day. This book is packed with biblical, practical, inspiring wisdom. Read this book, and then buy a bunch for your friends."

Mark Roberts, senior pastor, Irvine Presbyterian Church

"Tod Bolsinger wants you to be comfortable and convincing when taking your Christian faith out in public. He takes us along with him in his own journey of learning how to 'make a sermon walk.' This is a book to be read with relish, chewed on in discussion groups, and digested slowly for its nutritious value in growing weak faith into strong love."

Ray S. Anderson, senior professor of theology and ministry, Fuller Theological Seminary

"The apostle Peter was talking to *you*! In specific, clear, easy-to-understand language that can be understood and acted upon two thousand years later, with good humor and wonderful illustrations Tod Bolsinger unpacks the practical, life-changing directions Christ's 'rock' laid out. Do yourself, your family, and your friends a great spiritual favor: buy and read this book."

Hugh Hewitt, columnist, host of *The Hugh Hewitt Show*

SHOWTIME

LIVING DOWN HYPOCRISY
BY LIVING OUT THE FAITH

TOD BOLSINGER

BakerBooks
Grand Rapids, Michigan

For Al and Enid . . .

for all you do every day
to show Jesus to everyone.

© 2004 by Tod Bolsinger

Published by Baker Books
a division of Baker Publishing Group
P.O. Box 6287, Grand Rapids, MI 49516-6287
www.bakerbooks.com

Printed in the United States of America

Library of Congress Cataloging-in-Publication Data
Bolsinger, Tod E.
    Show time : living down hypocrisy by living out the faith / Tod
Bolsinger.
        p.   cm.
    Includes bibliographical references.
    ISBN 0-8010-6508-9 (pbk.)
    1. Christian life—Meditations. I. Title.
BV4501.3.B6554 2004
248.4—dc22   2004013962

CONTENTS

FOREWORD

While I was chaplain of the United States Senate, I admired the strength and steadfastness of Senator Pete Domenici as he proposed and fought for the passage of what was called the "Character Counts" legislation. It designated the third week of October "Character Counts Week" in America. Teachers across the land were encouraged to instruct their students about what were called the six pillars of character: trustworthiness, respect, responsibility, fairness, caring, and citizenship. The legislation was passed with enthusiasm and was renewed in subsequent legislation each year. The senators wanted to be sure that character was taught in our schools.

One year, in all five of the Bible studies sponsored by the Chaplain's Office, we considered one character pillar a week. A senator remarked, "Passing character legislation doesn't assure character development. I'm glad we did it, but I find it impossible to really live these character traits without God's help." Throughout the Bible studies, we were brought back to the assurance that God has revealed his character in Christ and wants to perform a character transplant in us. The challenge of living as a Christian in today's culture is making that the primary goal of our lives.

Here's a book that will really help.

You are about to read a very exciting book from the poignant and penetrating pen of one of America's most effective pastors and stimulating authors. Tod Bolsinger's *Show Time: Living Down Hypocrisy by Living Out the Faith* is a stunning contemporary communication of the biblical call for character.

This book came out of the profound dialogue between Dr. Bolsinger and his members at San Clemente Presbyterian Church. It was his people's struggles and successes in living out their faith among their families, on the job, and in the soul-sized issues of living authentically in contemporary culture that pressed Pastor Bolsinger to preach and teach from this portion of 2 Peter. But his preparation for writing this excellent book did not stop there. He engaged his people in deep personal conversations to test each chapter's relevance to those whose duty is to live out every day a down-to-earth quality of faith-motivated character.

I like the way he put it: "This book was born of the pain of Christians who have had to 'live down' the inconsistent lives of other believers. . . . So much of the hypocrisy of the church results from our tendency to wear two faces: our church face and our real face. Sooner or later, the real face takes over."

Bolsinger helps us to be sure that our lives are true reflections of authentic Christ-motivated character. The virtues produced by faith—goodness, knowledge, self-control, endurance, godliness, mutual affection, and love—"are to be put to use in real-life situations," he writes, "so that other people will come to the knowledge of Jesus Christ."

In a very compelling way, he explains and illustrates the dynamics of character listed in 2 Peter. I've not read a finer contemporary exposition of these verses. Bolsinger's working knowledge of biblical Greek, his historical scholarship, his keen understanding of the demands and delights of discipleship, and his genuine love for struggling, sometimes stumbling, Christians combine to make this a very inspiring book.

Eric Liddle, an Olympic champion who was depicted in the movie *Chariots of Fire*, said, "When I run fast, I feel the Lord's pleasure."

This book will help you run with the Master fast and free and experience his pleasure. It is time for Christians to show the world true character. Indeed, it is show time!

Lloyd J. Ogilvie

ACKNOWLEDGMENTS

Like my calling as a pastor and my life as a Christian, this book has been from start to finish a community endeavor. It began as sermons given to San Clemente Presbyterian Church, where I serve as senior pastor. I developed the series in response to questionnaires that my congregation filled out. They indicated a desire for some sermons that "applied Christianity to everyday living." The tapes of those sermons remain the highest-selling series at our church.

The sermons were then rewritten for my Wednesday morning men's small group, who gave me not only ample feedback but in some cases blunt correction. They were then completely overhauled numerous more times through frank conversations with Christian men and women who cared more about what Christianity should mean in the real world than my pride as an author. To all of these friends, I am grateful. While I will not name all of them, courtesy and a desire to give due credit necessitates that I name a few.

Not a day goes by that I don't give thanks to God for the privilege and joy of being pastor of San Clemente

Presbyterian Church. The people of this wonderful community genuinely love each other, are eager to grow in Christ, and are exceedingly patient with their pastor. They love me and my family. They encourage my writing, and by their sincere desire to live out the Christian faith before the eyes of their friends and neighbors, they inspired this book.

Two small groups read the manuscript and discussed all of the questions in the book. The first I have already mentioned, a group of men who for the better part of six years met with me every Wednesday morning to talk about living out the faith. A second small group, led by my friend Mike Bollenbacher, also read the book from start to finish and invited me to join them one Saturday morning for some really good coffee and even better discussion. I consider these friends experts in living as Christians in their families, in the marketplace, and in civic arenas. Their struggles and successes pushed me to express the teaching of 2 Peter 1:3–11 in terms that are relevant to everyday Christians.

The book itself was nurtured along and made stronger through friends, pastors, and literary experts who graciously and generously offered feedback and asked probing questions. When I was stuck for the first time in the awkward transition from spoken sermons to book format, Rob Asghar offered editorial assistance and served as a sounding board over lunches and through email. My friend Mark Roberts read the whole manuscript in an early stage and gave pointed feedback and gracious encouragement. I am most indebted to Mark for launching me on the way to a writing ministry. My friend and mentor Lloyd Ogilvie also read the book in its entirety, and (as his life and ministry have done for decades) he reminded me of the importance of the witness of lay leaders who live for Christ and our work as pastors to support them.

Don Stephenson and Chad Allen of Baker Books helped me to better express the vision of this book for a wider audience. Chad is that rare editor who can inspire an author to rewrite a favorite chapter and then feel all the better for it. His enthusiasm for this project was exceeded only by his ability to listen well, his keen editorial eye, and his prayerful confidence that God could use this book for good.

To my wife, Beth, and children Brooks and Alison, you are the well holding the grace and love of God that springs fresh each day. I draw nourishment for my soul and joy for my life because of the privilege of spending every day with you in this wonderful adventure of life. I love you deeply.

The people who are most deserving of acknowledgment are the men and women whose stories are found within this book, especially those personal friends who never dreamt that their lives would be chronicled publicly. They generously let me do so. I am honored to know you all. I am particularly grateful to Al and Enid Sloan and the example they are every single day to my family and me. Al and Enid, if I can preach one sermon with as much integrity, passion, devotion, and joy that you exhibit with your lives each day, I will be faithful to my calling. When Beth and I grow up, we want to be like you. Because of the way your lives "show and tell" the faith, this book is dedicated to you.

INTRODUCTION

"Sometimes I think Christians should just shut up."

He wasn't mad, just resigned. He said it with more of a sigh than with spite. Mick is a committed Christian, a successful builder, a good friend. We were talking about the difficulties of living out the Christian faith in the world and had run through the usual litany of challenges: bias against religion, ethical relativism, the temptation to cut corners.

But then Mick surprised me.

"You know, Tod, my biggest problem with telling people I'm a Christian is other Christians."

Mick added that his non-Christian business partner once told him, "Whenever someone tells me he is a Christian in the middle of a deal, I guard my wallet. You want me to take your faith seriously, but I keep running into Christians who preach Jesus but don't live like him."

Mick's wife, Shari, a pharmaceutical sales rep, chimed in. "Whenever a new person joins our group on the sales team and tells people that he or she is a Christian, everyone looks at me. They ask, 'Is she legit, or is this just another one of those Bible thumpers?' Everybody has a story of some Christian who crammed Jesus down their throats and yet couldn't do the job."

If you're like my friends, you are gun shy when it comes to talking about your faith. You want your words about Jesus to be taken seriously, yet you know that not everyone who talks about Jesus deserves being taken seriously. You want to be different from those who spend more time talking about their faith than living it. You want your life to share the gospel before you've even said a word. After all, talk is cheap, and more people should take to heart the legendary words attributed to St. Francis: "Preach the gospel at all times; use words when necessary."

Why Read This Book?

This book is for Christians who have had to live down the hypocrisy of others who did not live out their faith. Using one biblical passage, 2 Peter 1:3–11, we will take a journey to genuine faith that confronts and overcomes this frustrating form of public Christianity. This biblical passage teaches us about living a life that reveals Christ and commends him to unbelievers—a life that shows before it tells.

Ultimately, this book is about displaying through our increasingly transformed lives the grace of God given to us in Jesus Christ. It is for those who want the way they live to speak to their loved ones, colleagues, and friends. It is for Christians who are painfully aware of how often most believers—including themselves—fail to live up to the call and example of Christ.

If you're like me, you believe the good news that Jesus Christ offers everyone. You want your friends to respond to Christ's invitation to eternal life. You live every day surrounded by people whom you genuinely care about but who really don't understand what your commitment to Jesus Christ means to you—or what it could mean to them. You're weary of Christian caricatures on television. You're tired of seeing people roll their eyes when someone mentions Jesus.

Let's face it. Our world is wary of words without deeds. While President Bush was flying around in *Air Force 1* making statements immediately after the September 11th attacks, people criticized him. They picked at his words and parsed his phrases. No matter what he said, he couldn't get it right. But when he went to Ground Zero, grabbed a bullhorn, and stood amid the smoking rubble, surrounded by rescue workers and grieving family members, the whole country stopped to listen. It almost didn't matter what he said. The fact that the leader of the free world had come down to stand in the pain was comforting and inspiring. Simple words and consistent actions were what won the president respect that day.

And that same approach is what the world needs from the followers of Christ: simple words, consistent actions. Believers who proclaim with their lips and demonstrate with their lives the good news of God. Disciples who both show and tell the gospel. But as my friends Mick and Shari would insist, some of us should stop telling until our lives show the difference that Christ makes.

Making a Difference

A story circulated in Detroit about the early days of Henry Ford and the Ford Motor Company. It concerned a machinist who over a period of years had "borrowed" tools from the plant. Although it was against company policy, everybody did it, and management did nothing about it.

One day, however, the machinist was converted. He was baptized and took his baptism seriously. The day after, he gathered all the tools he had collected over the years, loaded them into his pickup, took them to the plant, and presented them to the foreman with his confession and a request for forgiveness.

The foreman was so overcome by the man's honesty that he cabled Henry Ford himself, who was traveling in Europe. After the foreman explained the event in detail, the story goes, Ford cabled back. "Dam up the Detroit River," he said, "and baptize the entire plant."

The world is yearning to see the difference a true, effective, and fruitful faith can make. The world is longing to see the gospel demonstrated in our lives with as much passion and vigor as we proclaim it with our lips. The world needs to meet people like my friends Al and Enid.

Al and Enid are members of my church. After Al completed a successful career as president of a large real-estate company in Southern California, they retired to a condo overlooking the ocean in our beach town. They had planned well and retired comfortably. They were in good health and were eager to travel. They had achieved the world's definition of success, and no one would have begrudged them a desire to spend their twilight years basking in their achievements and living in prosperity.

Now, Al and Enid have always been involved in ministry. Numerous pastors and missionaries serving throughout the world were once part of their youth group when they were sponsors. But it has been during their retirement years that they have truly made an impact. Though they easily could have chosen to spend the rest of their years enjoying worldly success, Al and Enid have touched many people by preaching the gospel with their lives.

Enid has been a mentor to many women, a trained caregiver to people in crisis, and a deacon bringing the love and care of the church to people in her neighborhood.

Al was part of the search committee that called me as pastor. After I settled into my new job, he came to me and said, "Tod, I have maybe ten good years left, and I want to make a difference for Christ." We talked over lunch one day, and he joined our church staff as an unpaid director of lay ministries. His job was to inspire and mobilize our congregation to service. And what a job he did. As a result of his efforts, over 90 percent of our congregation filled out gifts-discernment surveys and then through Al's leading found meaningful ways to serve. On our first lay-ministry appreciation celebration, over five hundred names were listed among those who had served during the year.

But Al and Enid didn't stop there. Putting his business acumen to work, Al taught our church staff how to be more efficient in strategic planning. Together, Al and Enid reinvigorated our church's prayer ministry, enlisting over six hundred people to pray every day for the church's staff and lay leadership, writing daily prayer devotionals for teachers in our church and reorganizing a telephone and email prayer chain. All the while, they kept caring for and encouraging a young minister who was in his first call as senior pastor.

Al and Enid have inspired the people in our church to serve with gusto and wisdom, and they have received a lot of recognition. But even our congregants don't know the half of it. After Easter, Al and Enid often take lilies left over from the service to shut-ins. When we had a building campaign, they sacrificed three years of fun vacations in order to give generously to the project. Enid leads a spiritual formation group for women and regularly visits an elderly invalid at least once a week.

17

Al takes ice cream to a neighbor in his nineties, also a shut-in, who had never professed faith. For months, while eating the treat Al brought, they watched the *Jesus* film together.

When another elderly man named Andy became invalid, Al became a daily source of support to him. Andy's wife had died a few months earlier, and he had no family to look after him. Al took over his affairs. He organized a crew of people to clean out his condominium, saw that it was sold for a fair price, paid all the bills, haggled with health-insurance companies, got Andy placed in a comfortable nursing home, and visited him every day until he finally died in peace, holding the hand of a nurse who was a member of our church. For months afterward, Al took care of Andy's estate and saw that Andy's wishes were carried out. As Andy's pastor, I was stunned when I found out that this quiet little man had left over $150,000 to our church as a token of his appreciation for the care given to him by our church elder and his good friend Al.

When my own aunt Dorothy McPhillips died, my brother said about her, "If more people were Christians like her, more people would be Christians." That's the way that I feel about Al and Enid. I think Mick and Shari and all my other friends would want those very words said about them someday. I know I would. Don't we all? Ultimately, lives that effectively "preach the gospel at all times" are what faith is all about.

FAITH
THAT WORKS

Frustrations in Faith and Fly-Fishing

A few years ago, my wife and I took our two children on a ten-day vacation in the Canadian Rockies. Some old friends joined us, and we tooled around in two rented RVs, looking for elk, bears, waterfalls, and glaciers. As we went, everyone put up with my penchant for seeking out fishing holes.

For me one of the trip's highlights was that I finally was able to use the fly rod that my staff had given to me as a gift for completing my Ph.D. Five-weight, four-piece, great action—it's a beauty. My friend Rob and I got up early one morning, piled into one of the RVs, and headed out of Jasper National Park to the Fraser River below Mount Robson in British Columbia. There we met our guide, who had promised to turn us into fly-fishing fanatics. We looked forward to fulfilling the adage "Give a man a fish, and he'll eat dinner one night; teach him to fish, and he'll be late for dinner every night."

Our guide was an earnest young guy who had plenty of experience and was eager to show us his skill. He offered me a rod to borrow; I scoffed and pulled out my new bad boy. Trout beware.

But the first place we went, we struck out. (Even the guide!) So we decided to try a little lake. Two hours later, we had nothing but stories of the *several* that got away. We got hits; we even hooked a couple of pretty small ones—we just couldn't seem to reel them in. It was both fun and frustrating. I may have had a brand-new rod, but it was painfully obvious that I didn't know how to use it very well.

As we drove home, we realized that while our guide was a good guy, his youth probably made him intimidated by us. (Only more so, I think, when he found out that his two students were a pastor and a lawyer.) He was supportive and encouraging, but he didn't offer much in the way of instruction, correction, and teaching. He had tried really hard to impress us with his ability, but he hadn't really done all that much to improve ours.

I figured there must be about a thousand tips he didn't tell us. I found myself wishing we could have another day on the water with an old fisherman. You know, some old guy who has failed so much that he now rarely does, who's forgotten more than I'll ever know, isn't afraid to tell me what I am doing wrong, and, especially, could help me figure out how to make this brand-new rod really *work*.

I hate things that don't work. I know, *hate* is a strong word. But many of you will understand. Let's say you get a brand-new laptop computer. You are looking forward to new power, new speed, to surfing through the World Wide Web like a long-boarder on a deserted Hawaiian break. You can't wait for the ability to crunch numbers, generate a spreadsheet, fire off a memo, and order Chinese takeout all at the same time. You can really get to *work.*

You take it out of the box, set it up; it hums right along, the screen flickers, the words scroll across the screen. Ahh . . . some new gear. A new gizmo. You happily start putting it to good use, all the while laughing at the instructions sitting in the box, like you're in a present-day version of the *Treasures of Sierra Madre*: "Manuals? We don't need no stinking manuals!"

And all is going well until . . . a button sticks. The cursor doesn't respond. The program freezes. A message flashes on the screen: "Fatal Error, Fatal Error." "Argh!" you shriek. "Either something's wrong with this thing, or something's wrong with me."

For many of us, this kind of experience is similar to our experience of faith. It all started out so promisingly. We had such peace, such power, such a sense of having a direct line to God. Then, a glitch here, something gets stuck there. The same Bible that once seemed interesting now puts us to sleep. Our prayers bounce off the ceiling and crash down on our heads. We feel like we're talking into a void. Our patience is waning; we are tempted by old desires and overwhelmed by what feel like unconquerable struggles. Soon we are ready to compromise the very things we claim are most important. If we had a diagnostic tool, we fear it would say, "Fatal Error." We think to ourselves, *Either something's wrong with this Christianity thing or something's wrong with me.*

You deeply want a faith that helps you make a difference in the hurly-burly of everyday life. You especially want a faith that makes a noticeable difference—a difference that others will notice—but your faith seems ineffective at best, a downright disappointment at worst. After trying to do it on your own, perhaps you are now looking for a guide, a teacher, an old fisherman.

Let me introduce you to the apostle Peter.

Learning from an Old Fisherman

The book of 2 Peter is attributed to the chief disciple of Jesus, Simon, whom Jesus called Peter. By most scholarly accounts, this book was probably written for Peter by one of his disciples who edited his many teachings. Don't get me wrong. I believe Peter is the author. But Peter was a fisherman, a man of deeds, not words. Somebody wanted to write a tribute to the old fisherman and premier apostle that encapsulated his final teaching, so this person, this scribe, edited the teachings of Peter into something like his last words or a final testament of wisdom to be passed down to a new generation. The language of 2 Peter is that of a learned ghostwriter who was making sure that his mentor's effective real-world faith was communicated clearly. This was as common then as it is today, and the subtle message woven throughout the letter is indeed a tribute: "Peter didn't just teach this stuff; he lived it. His most powerful message was his life. And from him you can learn to live the faith."

This letter starts with greetings and a prologue that sets the stage, and then the main section of the first chapter, verses 5–7, features a list of character qualities. After the list is a summary of the benefits of having such qualities, followed by a warning and then an encouragement.

For this study, I will often refer to two different translations of 2 Peter 1:3–11. One is the New Revised Standard Version:

> His divine power has given us everything needed for life and godliness, through the knowledge of him who called us by his own glory and goodness. Thus he has given us, through these things, his precious and very great promises, so that through them you may escape

from the corruption that is in the world because of lust, and may become participants of the divine nature. For this very reason, you must make every effort to support your faith with goodness, and goodness with knowledge, and knowledge with self-control, and self-control with endurance, and endurance with godliness, and godliness with mutual affection, and mutual affection with love. For if these things are yours and are increasing among you, they keep you from being ineffective and unfruitful in the knowledge of our Lord Jesus Christ. For anyone who lacks these things is nearsighted and blind, and is forgetful of the cleansing of past sins. Therefore, brothers and sisters, be all the more eager to confirm your call and election, for if you do this, you will never stumble. For in this way, entry into the eternal kingdom of our Lord and Savior Jesus Christ will be richly provided for you.

But I also want to offer a translation of my own. Not unlike Peter's first-century scribe, I want to capture some of the nuances of the original phrases in contemporary language. As I have been mentored by Peter's teaching and life, I want my contemporaries to learn from him also. So compare my own paraphrase of this passage with the NRSV:

Because in Jesus Christ you have all the power you need to live well and in a manner worthy of God, and because through trusting in his promises you are freed from the polluting bondage that holds the world captive, you must use that godly power to produce from your faith everything that you need for life:

From your faith, produce virtue that is commendable by the world's best standards.
From your virtue, produce a wisdom that can apply that virtue in real-world situations.

From your wisdom, produce a self-control that can enjoy freedom in Christ while knowing safe limits.

From that inner strength, produce endurance to face whatever challenge arises before you.

Let this constancy of character reveal integrity of actions and beliefs, both in worship and in life, and especially in the Community of Faith, through loving vulnerability and generous mercy.

Last, let all that is produced through your faith lavishly and consistently overflow in redemptive love to everyone in your life.

If these traits are part of your walk and increasingly so, you will never be ineffective and unfruitful in knowing our Lord Jesus, the Messiah. But beware! If you neglect these things, you are walking blindly on the edge of a cliff, forgetting that only God's gracious forgiveness has brought you safely to this place in the journey. Therefore, my brothers and sisters, put your faith to work in the real world and demonstrate that it is indeed genuine. If you do this, you will never stumble as you live as a citizen of God's kingdom now and forever.

Faith and Love

As you can see, the center of this passage is a list of character qualities. Throughout history, people have made lists of virtues, as well as vices, for the sake of moral instruction. Such lists are prominent in the philosophy of Stoicism, which began under Zeno (340–265 BC) and was the dominant worldview in the first-century world that Peter addressed.[1] Philosophers like Philo (ca. 20 BC–AD 50), Seneca (ca. 4 BC–AD 65), Epictetus (ca. AD 50–130), and Plutarch (AD 50–120) all made abundant use of these lists in their teaching. In American history, both Benjamin Franklin and George Washington worked their entire lives on well-known lists that they presumably used to stimulate their character development.

In most cases, the writings of the New Testament adopted and then adapted Greco-Roman lists to reflect Christian values. Thirteen lists of virtues appear in the New Testament, all but two of which are found in Epistles:

2 Corinthians 6:6–8
Galatians 5:22–23
Ephesians 4:32; 5:9
Philippians 4:8
Colossians 3:12
1 Timothy 4:12; 6:11
2 Timothy 2:22; 3:10
James 3:17
1 Peter 3:8
2 Peter 1:5–7[2]

If we were to diagram Peter's list, it might look like a set of stairs that starts in the lofty heights of faith and descends, with each virtue leading to the next, until the list ends in the down-to-earth expression of love:

Faith producing virtue
Virtue producing wisdom
Wisdom producing self-control
Self-control producing endurance
Endurance producing godliness
Godliness producing mutual affection
Mutual affection producing love

Note that in the ancient world, the first and last words in lists like this were the most important. Our list in

2 Peter begins with *faith* and ends with *love*. The writer is telling us that of all the items in this whole glorious list, we are to focus first on faith and last on love. Or in the words of St. Ignatius, "If you be perfect in your faith and love toward Jesus Christ, . . . these are the beginning and end of life—faith is the beginning and love is the end."[3] Paul emphasizes this point even more clearly in Galatians 5:6 when he writes, "The only thing that counts is faith working through love" (NRSV).

Nothing New

If you read the whole letter of 2 Peter (and you could do so in one short sitting), you can almost hear the pathos, the pleading. It sounds like it was written by someone who saw many people excitedly make great confessions of faith but then end up stumbling so badly that they contradicted the faith they claimed. We read in 2 Peter 1 an admonition to "support your faith" by developing character, by cultivating virtue, by expressing with our lives the qualities that speak effectively to others. We are taught that faith is effective when character is being produced in our lives—when we are people who not only confess faith in Christ but also reflect Christ through virtue, wisdom, self-control, endurance, godliness, affection, and love.

This catalog of admirable qualities ends in a verse that seems to jump right off the page: "For if these things are yours and are increasing among you, they keep you from being ineffective and unfruitful in the knowledge of our Lord Jesus Christ" (v. 8 NRSV).

Notice that this is written to believers, those who have knowledge of our Lord Jesus Christ, a fact which becomes even clearer if you look at verse 2. But here the writer says that his intention is to help believers keep from being ineffective and unfruitful. In other words, this is written to Christians whose faith is not working like they know it should. It is written to those of us whose faith is not causing the good effects that Christian faith should inspire, who are not producing the fruit of godliness in their lives, whose lives are preaching a different gospel than their lips.

Ineffective. Unfruitful. Strong words. But perhaps they are accurate words for most of us. We are believers. We know Jesus Christ as Lord and Savior. We have been baptized, we have confessed our faith, and we may even have had miraculous life-transforming moments. But something nags us: *Is this all there is? If I have faith, why does it seem like I make so little difference in my family, my job, my community? If Christianity is the truth that gives us life eternal and abundant, then why doesn't it seem to work the way I hoped it would? Why don't people who are hurting seek me out? Why don't friends who need hope ask me about my hope in Christ? Why is my faith so . . . ineffective and unfruitful?*

According to some recent statistics, there are two billion Christians in the world today. Fully one-third of the world's population confesses faith in Christ. So let me ask you, When you read the headlines of the *Los Angeles Times* or the *Washington Post*, do you see much evidence of that? Or how about this: 80 percent of the people in Orange County, California, where I live, claim to be Christians. Eighty percent![4] Maybe I just expect too much, but doesn't it seem like all this Christian faith in the world is "ineffective and unfruitful"?

Well, this isn't just a contemporary problem. Imagine, if you will, that you are living late in the first century. You are a disciple of Peter, and you can remember his martyr's death in Rome. You remember what it felt like when you heard that your mentor, the old fisherman, the great apostle, the all-too-human but oh-so-passionate Simon

Peter, was dead. The Roman authorities sentenced him to die on a cross like the Lord he loved, but he declared he was not worthy to die like Jesus did and insisted on being crucified upside down.

Such commitment. Such passion. Such a witness to the power of trusting Christ. Just the way he lived inspired people to emulate him—even you. His faith was so relevant, so real.

Peter's life was a mixed bag, you remember. He first met Jesus on a boat, where Jesus outfished him with a miraculous catch, and he ended up face down, asking for mercy. He was the guy who confessed Jesus as Lord before anybody else did. And he was the one who failed miserably by denying Christ the night he was crucified. Peter had spent hours telling you and his other disciples all those stories. The story of his faith, the story of his failure. The story of confessing, the story of denying. Peter knew all about stumbling, about failing, about the frustration of knowing Christ and still not living faithfully to Christ. Yet in the end, because of his faith, he was faithful. His life was effective, and in you it had borne fruit.

But when you take a look around, you see people who are taking the message of faith and turning it into a license to sin. They look at faith as a Get Out of Hell Free card that they stick in their pockets and forget about until they die. They are neglecting the life of discipleship, the joyful and narrow path of following Christ in daily life. Oh, many are confessing their faith, enamored by the message of grace displayed in the life of the Carpenter from Nazareth, but so few are living it like he did. And you see the cynicism of unbelievers who scoff at the idea that this new religion makes any difference at all.

So you pick up your quill and papyri and write a tribute, a collection of Peter's teachings, things you heard him say, with some light editing of your own. With the inspiration of the Spirit, you pass on Peter's teaching to

Christians who are stumbling all around you. And you try to drive home a central thought: *faith is not something you have; it's something you do.*

Faith That Works

The purpose of faith is to let God's power and presence flow from God into your life and through your life into others. For faith to work, it must be put to work, and not just in churches and Bible studies but in boardrooms and classrooms, at kitchen tables and in police stations, and in intimate family moments that no one else sees.

In Peter's letter, we learn about faith that makes a difference. Faith that is effective and fruitful. Faith that not only takes us to the mountaintop, giving us spiritual goose bumps and tears in our eyes, but also causes us to roll up our sleeves and return to the real world of human need. Faith that brings God's love, compassion, and truth to bear on the world around us.

To have that kind of faith—faith that works—we need to understand that (1) it depends on God's work and power, (2) it requires our trust, and (3) it results in our living it out. Let's look at each of these.

1. Faith that works depends on God's work and power. As we in California learned a few years ago during several long, statewide blackouts, you can have the best transmission lines in the world, but if energy stops coming from the source, blackouts follow. Everything starts with the power source. In the same way, all genuine virtue and change in life depend on God's work and power in our lives. In verse 3 we read, "His divine power has given us everything needed for life and godliness, through the knowledge of him who called us" (NRSV). In other words, showing and telling the Christian life is not the result of any virtue, talent, or ability of our own.

Instead, it is the public demonstration of what God has been doing in our lives since the moment he graciously gave us eternal life.

Note that "preaching the gospel with our lives" begins not with our lives but with the gospel. All effective faith must rest on and daily demonstrate our deep awareness that, left to ourselves, we would never live one effective Christ-displaying day ever. Left to ourselves, we would never seek God. Left to ourselves, we would never be transformed one bit. And all effective faith begins with that knowledge and rests and relies on God's grace and power in our lives, which leads to the second point.

2. Faith that works requires our trust. It may sound simplistic, but effective faith must be genuine trust, and genuine trust is living in complete and utter dependence on the grace and mercy of God every day. Effective faith is not about depending on God's grace for salvation and then doing the best we can on our own steam; it is faith that displays the trust we have in God's grace for our salvation by living it out. Effective faith demonstrates that we know that we have been "saved by grace through faith" (Eph. 2:8 NRSV) and then in awe-filled gratitude to God seeks to demonstrate the difference that that knowledge makes.

Second Peter 1:4 reads, "Thus he has given us . . . his precious and very great promises, so that through them you may escape from the corruption that is in the world" (NRSV). Notice that we are transformed and faith works in us "through" trusting God's promises. Only through that trusting faith do we "escape from the corruption that is in the world." Only through faith are we saved and become believers. This trusting is what makes us different from the world. No matter how much we may focus on our efforts to display the Christian life, we can't leave behind the requirement of trusting God in Christ. All attempts to teach values or character devoid of faith fall short. If we want Christianity to make a difference in the world, each person who claims to be a Christian must in fact trust Christ for salvation and live each day demonstrating the difference genuine faith in Christ makes; this takes us to our last point.

3. *Faith that works results in our living it out.* For some of us, all this talk about work and faith gives us the theological heebie-jeebies. Isn't faith the opposite of works? Isn't the point of faith that our efforts are worthless, that we can't really do anything? Isn't that what Ephesians 2:8–9 means when it says we are saved by faith and not by works?

I once heard Dallas Willard make a helpful comment. He said, "Grace is opposed not to effort but to earning." We cannot earn our salvation through our works, but grace does inspire us to work. It inspires us to faith-filled effort.

Which brings us to the crux of this passage.

Show Time

Verse 5 includes an interesting and often confusing sentence. It reads, "You must make every effort to support your faith with goodness" (NRSV). At first glance, this seems to be saying, "Do all you can to add goodness to your faith." It seems to imply that faith, pure and simple, isn't really enough. A quick read through the passage may lead us to think that effective faith is really "faith plus a whole list of virtues." But that is not what is meant by the word for support here. It is not about adding to our faith; it is about providing evidence for our faith the way a courtroom witness "supports" the truth by testifying to it. It's about expressing the genuineness of our faith by living it out.

This meaning becomes even clearer when we consider that the word for support here is a word that was used of wealthy patrons who paid for an acting troupe's costumes and equipment. Picture a troupe that has been lavishly equipped with all they need to perform. This text tells us that God outfits and equips us with goodness and all the other character qualities in the same way that a patron equips a group of actors.[5] Then God the patron demands that we put on a show that puts to use all that he has graciously provided. In other words, we are to make every effort to put on and put to use the very character of God that he has put into our lives.

This image of a patron equipping actors to display what he has given them is the central image of the text, the key metaphor. We are to "support" the veracity and reality of the faith we have in Christ by "showing" it through increasingly virtuous character. We are not trying to earn the approval or acceptance of God by doing so, but we are to express or demonstrate to a watching world that we have been graciously accepted by God.

From beginning to end, God is the one who provides the faith, and we believers are to put that faith on display like an acting troupe puts on a performance. Paul says something similar in Philippians 2:12–13: "Work out your own salvation with fear and trembling; for it is God who is at work in you, enabling you both to will and to work for his good pleasure" (NRSV). Or as one of my seminary professors once put it, "We work *out* what God has worked *in* us."[6]

One More Word about Effort

G. K. Chesterton once said, "Christianity has not been tried and found wanting; it has been found difficult and left untried." And maybe in the final analysis that is why faith is so often ineffective and unfruitful. We really don't try it fully. We talk a good game, we accept the grace that God has poured into our lives, but we don't really commit ourselves to living out the gospel. We want to be people of character who are respected by others, but we don't dedicate ourselves to allowing God's transforming power to work in every area of our lives—because, frankly, that takes work.

I know that all this discussion about work and effort can be discouraging. It just feels, well, tiring. And most of us have plenty of work to do. We don't want to work. We want our faith in Christ to make our lives easier, less work. But let me help you think about this differently.

Yes, developing character is difficult work, and it takes effort, but it's not labor. It's art. Throughout ancient history, there always has been a strong tie between ethics and aesthetics. Historically, what was truly beautiful was also morally good. Increasing in godly character as this passage describes is not drudgery but passionate action. It is bringing forth and putting on display the beauty of God in the way we live.

Living out our faith is like being a musician who dedicates himself to notes and scales to express the song that has captured his heart. It's like being a painter who looks intently at color and light, disciplining her hand and eye to reveal the vision in her soul. It's like being a photographer who works at making a picture not just another snapshot but a poignant moment in this world. Or even a fly-fisherman creating the beauty of a fly rod moving between twelve and two in four-four time, casting the looping line into quietly moving water.

That's what first drew me to fly-fishing. The art of it. That's why I put in the effort to learn and grow as a fisherman. I wasn't inspired by a mental picture of me standing hip-deep in cold water, swatting mosquitoes while untangling my line from a tree. I was inspired by watching a man casting into the Madison River at Yellowstone as the sun went down and a herd of bison ambled by.

It is work, but it's inspired work, artistic work. Work that expresses something of the grace of God. To borrow the words that Malcolm Muggeridge used to describe Mother Teresa, it is the process of becoming "something beautiful for God."

In the classic fly-fishing story *A River Runs through It*, the narrator quotes his father, a fly-fishing Presbyterian pastor: "All good things—trout as well as eternal salvation—come by grace, and grace comes by art and art does not come easy."[7]

Questions to Consider

1. How do you feel when something important to you doesn't work? How do you respond?
2. Think of a time when you felt like your faith didn't work. What did you feel? What did you do?
3. With two billion professing Christians in the world, why doesn't faith make a bigger difference in the world?
4. Reread 2 Peter 1:3–11, especially verse 8. According to this passage, what do we need to be "effective and fruitful" in our knowledge of Jesus Christ?
5. What does it mean for you to "support" your faith (v. 5)? What do you need from God? What do you need to do to respond to God's power and promises?

FOR GOODNESS'
2 SAKE

For this very reason, you must make every effort to support your faith with goodness.

NRSV

From your faith, produce virtue that is commendable by the world's best standards.

author's translation

The Book of Virtues

One sunny afternoon in January 1993, I walked into my favorite bookstore in Pasadena, California, to be one of the first people to buy a book that had been released earlier in the day.

When I couldn't find the book on the new-releases shelf, I approached a clerk, who told me that the book had sold out within minutes of its release and that they did not expect to have any in stock for three months. I was shocked. I had been looking forward to buying it, but I didn't think anyone else was. This wasn't any

Tom Clancy thriller or Jackie Collins romance. It wasn't a tell-all political biography or a book on how to make millions in the stock market. It wasn't *The Prayer of Jabez* or *Left Behind.* It was a $28, eight-hundred-page collection of stories.

I thought the only people who would buy it would be preachers like me, those who live each week desperate for a sermon illustration. I could not have been more wrong.

This thick storybook instantly became and long remained a *New York Times* bestseller. It sold in excess of three million copies; it inspired sequels for children and young adults that have sold nearly two million copies. It spawned a PBS television show and thrust the author into the limelight. His name was often batted around as a potential candidate for every office in our land, including president. The name of this storybook? *The Book of Virtues.*

Interesting, isn't it? When we talk about being good or virtuous, many of us fear that we will become the object of someone else's cynical remarks. We remember all too well what happened to our playmates on the playground who were considered a goody two-shoes.

But I believe that deep within all of us is a genuine desire to be good. In an interview in *Vanity Fair*, humorist Garrison Keillor sounded a note of disillusionment that is all too common these days: "My generation strikes me as self-absorbed. You hear them at the grocery store deliberating over the balsamic vinegar and the olive oils . . . and you think, 'These people probably subscribe to an olive-oil magazine called 'New Dimension.' They are people with too much money and very little character, people who are all sensibility and no sense, all nostalgia and no history, the people my Aunt Eleanor used to call a $10 haircut on a 59-cent head—people I would call yuppie swine."[1]

36

Like Garrison Keillor, I believe that many of us fear that our children are doomed to self-absorbed childishness. We look at the famous and see few heroes about, few lives worth emulating. We are becoming weary from the waste of powerful leaders whose personal peccadilloes become the punch lines for another late-night monologue. Despite all of David Letterman's smirks, we are hungry to see the genuine article, to see someone who is really good.

I believe that this is a great opportunity for the church, if we have effective faith. Almost fifty years ago, Martin Lloyd-Jones wrote words that are even more accurate today: "If Christianity is what it claims to be, then it should be producing a type and order of life which is quite exceptional. If, therefore, we are to meet the challenge of the modern world we must be living the Christian life; and the question arises how we are to do so."[2]

This is exactly the question that 2 Peter aims to address. The first step for living an effective Christian life is to begin being transformed because we have been saved, not in order to be saved. This is why after recounting the power and promises available to believers so that they might "escape from the corruption that is in the world," Peter charges us to "make every effort to support your faith with goodness."

Now, if we translate this passage more literally, it reads, "Express your faith with virtue." So the first lesson we need to learn if our lives are going to speak to people effectively and make a difference in the real world can be summarized by a concise charge: faith for the real world produces virtue, so be good and live better.

Be Good, Live Better

Peter is charging Christians who have been given the "imputed righteousness of Christ" (that is, have been declared good) through faith to become, in fact, more righteous (that is, to increase in goodness). He is saying to us, "Since you have been declared virtuous, be virtuous, and as your faith deepens, express it in even more virtuous living."

Now, before we go any further, a word of caution is in order. When we talk about being good, we are not encouraging either perfectionism or legalism. Both are distortions of biblical virtue. When the Bible speaks of being virtuous, it is not exhorting people to live without flaw or to strictly adhere to a list of rules. But too often in the church today, those are the messages being taught.

The result is that far too many of us have struggled far too much with trying to be perfect; and far too many of us have expressed self-righteousness, not virtue. But neither the word nor the implication in the passage is about achieving perfection or keeping rules. Instead, in verse 8, Peter sums up the entire list by saying, "If these things are yours and are increasing among you, they keep you from being ineffective and unfruitful" (NRSV). He does not challenge us with perfectionism or rules-keeping but instead exhorts us to become people of a character that requires the steady, slow ripening of faith.

Virtue requires not perfection but maturity. Christian virtue is about being declared good and then consequently growing in goodness each day. But of course, this is easier said than done, so let me offer two suggestions for living out real-world Christian virtue.

1. Live Commendably

Are you familiar with the comic strip *Broom Hilda*? Broom Hilda is an ugly yet somehow lovable witch. Her friend Irwin is a troll whose innocence and naivete make him truly endearing.

One day Broom Hilda asks, "Irwin, what would be the best way to make the world a better place?"

Irwin thinks for a moment and replies, "Start with yourself! Give up your bad habits and evil pleasures. Then when you're good, you'll stand as a shining example to others!"

Uncomfortable with the answer, Broom Hilda responds, "What's the second best way?"

When our text urges us to support our faith with goodness, it is giving us the same advice. Effective faith begins not with trying to get others to be good but with being better people ourselves. It begins not with nagging others but with our expressing and increasing in the kind of virtuous living that is commendable to all people.

One of the most interesting things in this passage is Peter's choice of a word for goodness. He doesn't choose the usual word that signifies religious goodness or goodness that comes through obedience to God. Instead, he uses a word that shows up only one other time in New Testament character lists (Phil. 4:8). It is a more "secular" word, a philosophical word, the classic Greek word for virtue, *arête*.

In other words, we are to live lives that even those who don't believe in God will say are commendable ways of living. We need to live lives that even an unbeliever would respect. This is why I translate this phrase as "from your faith, produce virtue that is commendable by the world's best standards."

Again, the word *virtue* in Latin comes from the word *virtus*, from which we get the word *virility*. It means "manliness" and implies a kind of potency for living that inspires life as it is meant to be lived. Peter is saying that the church, the people of God, should demonstrate to the world how all humans are meant to live.

Unfortunately, the people of God seldom do. In their study of American Christianity, George Gallup Jr. and Jim Castelli identify what could be called an ethics gap in the church: the discrepancy between Christians' convictions and our consistency in living them out. They write, "While religion is highly popular in America, it is to a large extent superficial; it does not change people's lives to the degree one would expect from their level of professed faith."[3]

To give just one example, according to several studies by Christian researchers, evangelical Christians now have a slightly higher rate of divorce than non-Christians.[4] We who think of commitment, vows, and covenant relationships as part of the life of faith are simply not living as commendably as we avow we will.

Jesus often would goad religious people by holding up the example of those unbelievers who were by their actions better examples than believers. Consider, for example, the parable of the Good Samaritan in Luke 10. While the religious leaders of Jesus' day argued about who was worthy of one's care and concern ("Who is my neighbor?"), the despised mixed-race and theologically heterodox Samaritan in Jesus' parable acted with the kind of compassion and care that leads Jesus to exhort in Luke 10:37, "Go and do likewise." This would be like Billy Graham pointing to Gandhi and saying, "Do what he did!"

Throughout the New Testament, Christians are urged to commendable living.

> Live such good lives among the pagans that . . . they will see your good deeds and glorify God.
>
> 1 Peter 2:12 NIV

Let your light shine before others, so that they may see your good works and give glory to your Father in heaven.

Matthew 5:16 NRSV

Now let's be clear; this desired goodness doesn't come overnight, and books written and sermons preached won't instantly produce it. In *Mere Christianity*, C. S. Lewis compares becoming virtuous to becoming an athlete. He writes that even a bad tennis player might make a good shot now and then by sheer luck. But a truly good player is someone who has practiced making good shots for years: "Whose eye, muscles and nerves have been so trained . . . that they can now be relied on."[5] In the same way, someone who perseveres in doing what is right develops a reliable character. He or she regularly lives commendably and demonstrates over time Christ's goodness to a watching world.

Of course, virtue is not about putting our character on display to garner attention and praise. It is not about trying to make others think that we are a goody two-shoes. It is about living a morally good life whether we are noticed or not. As Dwight Moody once said, "Character is what you are in the dark."

Effective faith, therefore, is virtuous faith, and virtuous faith is living by standards that even unbelievers will commend. Like Mother Teresa, who won a Nobel Prize for doing the work of Jesus, it is about living with the kind of integrity and consistency of goodness that is admirable even to those who don't share our belief system.

2. Live Dependently

The second part to the definition is equally important, for virtuous faith is not only living commendably but also living dependently. Our text says, "Make every effort to support your faith with goodness" (NRSV). Once again, the word for support here does not mean to "add" to your faith, as some translations say, but "to produce through your faith." As I wrote in the previous chapter, it conjures up the image of a theater company putting on the costumes and using the props provided to them by a patron. Living virtuous faith is putting on the character that we have received through faith in Christ.

A second implication of this use of the word *arête*, or virtue, is that it is, once again, inextricably linked with faith. The Bible, contrary to the advice of well-intentioned people in the world, is teaching us that all true goodness can never be separated from faith in God.

For the classical Greeks, who have so pervasively influenced civilization for millennia, *virtue* represented the pinnacle of lists of human qualities. It usually refers to moral excellence brought about by human striving, which causes you to stand out as a greater human being worthy of praise, admiration, and emulation. It is the top of the ethical mountain.

In this biblical context, however, *arête* is not the pinnacle of but an early step in the journey, *after faith*. One commentator offers this helpful insight: "Despite the insistence in vv. 5–10 that faith must have moral results and that Christ's promises have ethical conditions, Peter is clear that salvation is not a human achievement. It is the grace of God that makes moral progress possible (vv. 3, 8)." Since this passage uses the ethical ideals of Greek civilization, it serves as an acknowledgment that even non-Christian societies have moral standards they hold up for admiration and emulation. However, Peter places them within the distinctively Christian attributes of faith and love, thereby declaring human self-improvement impossible without the work of Christ. The same commentator notes, "Christian faith is the root from which all virtues grow, and Christian love is the crowning virtue to which all the others must contribute."[6] Peter, while reminding us of the high calling of living virtuously, puts goodness *after* faith and changes the approach to attaining virtue in a radically spiritual direction.

Let me explain it this way. A couple of years ago when my family and I were in Jasper National Park in the Canadian Rockies, we made dinner reservations at a restaurant atop Mount Whistler. The views were said to be spectacular, though the food was barely edible.

Now, since we were eating at the top of a mountain, we had a decision to make: how do we get there? Some people hike the long and steep climb, spending the better part of the day and expending far more calories than they will want to consume at the buffet. Most opt instead to ride up the mountain in a gondola suspended from a steel cable. And that is what we did. We rode up the mountain, enjoyed a terrific view, laughed about the mediocre meal, and created memories that connected us more deeply as a family. It was a great day that reminded us all of how good our God is to have created such beautiful mountains and to have given us the chance to enjoy them together.

But now I must confess to you that left to myself, I would have rather hiked up that mountain than ridden the gondola. My inclination is to want to reach the top with a sense of accomplishment, of pride, of having used my own strength to conquer the mountain. I want to stand there panting and sweaty and beaming, taking in the view and thinking, if not outright saying, "Praise *me* for what I have done."

And the same is true of my moral life. Like climbers on Everest who want to make it to the summit without oxygen or die trying, I am tempted every day to try to live virtuously on my own steam, so that others will admire me and so that I can prove to myself that I am able to be righteous by myself.

Spiritually speaking, this is pure foolishness. It is impossible to climb the mountain of virtue by our own efforts. No one can ever make it. As Paul writes in Romans, "There is no one who is righteous, not even one; there is no one who has understanding, there is no one who seeks God. . . . all have sinned and fall short of the glory of God" (3:10–11, 23 NRSV).

What's worse is that in Hebrews 11:6, we learn that "without faith it is impossible to please God, for whoever would approach him must believe that he exists and that he rewards those who seek him" (NRSV). Therefore, even to attempt to live virtuously by our own efforts is to stumble backward down the mountain, not to make progress.

So now I and every other proud climber have a choice to make. Do we want to reach the summit or not? Are we willing to be taken where we cannot go? Are we willing to be made good by God, to ascend into the rare air of righteousness in the gondola of faith?

Make no mistake, to be a tram rider is inspiring—but in a different way. For as the rider comes off the gondola at the top of the mountain, he or she does not think, *Look what I have done*; instead, he or she thinks, *Praise be to you, O great and glorious God, for you not only have made all this beauty before us in all of its splendor but also have kept this tiny little box on this tiny little cable from falling out of the sky and killing us.*

Sure, tram riders have to put some effort into making their decision. They have to steel up some courage and trust that they will make it safely to the top. But they don't for one second think of themselves as worthy of praise. What for the hiker is a futile effort, for the rider is a fruitful exercise in faith. And that experience of trust begins the transformation to virtue.

You know, every time I come down from a summit, whether it is a stunning ski peak or a mediocre mountaintop restaurant, I find myself touching ground a bit more quietly, a bit more gingerly, even a bit more humbly than when I had left. Perhaps it is from having felt small and vulnerable hanging in midair. Perhaps it is from having spent some time basking in the majesty of mountains that jut into the sky like hands raised in worship. Or perhaps it is just the sense that every pinnacle in my life and everything I experience of goodness—whether it be a mountain peak, the heady air of a good day with my family, or a summit of faith—is a gift from God.

For the hiker striving for moral virtue, trying to summit in his or her own strength is the goal, even if the attempt is doomed to failure. But for those of us who arrive at the pinnacle of righteousness only through dependence on the power of God, goodness is the gratitude-inspired first step.

Virtue, Faith, and Love

For our lives to speak of the Good News, we must never forget that godly virtue comes from faith and leads to love. If our virtue doesn't, then it isn't godly virtue. Friends, let's not fall victim to well-intentioned striving for human goodness. All attempts at virtue apart from faith are flawed; all virtue apart from love fails. Produce faithful virtue by living commendably and living dependently.

Some of us, all too aware of the ways in which our lives have been anything but commendable, will wonder, Is it really possible for me to take even this first step? I am grateful that God has reached into my life through the grace of Jesus Christ and saved me from "the corruption that is in the world," but how can I really begin

45

to walk through life differently? How can I begin to take steps to live better? I try to confess Jesus with my lips, but how do I start speaking with my life?

One commentator puts it this way: "Progress in the Christian life is made possible and practical by two factors: the power of God and the promises of God."[7] The only way we are going to grow in expressing virtue in our lives is through God's work in us. Even before he starts his virtue list, Peter reminds us of this also. "Because in Jesus Christ you have all the power you need to live well and in a manner worthy of God, and because through trusting in his promises you are freed from the polluting bondage that holds the world captive" (author's translation).

In Philippians 1:6 we read words that tie together God's power and his promises. It is a very encouraging passage to those of us who wonder if we will ever be able to be good. "He who began a good work *among* you will be faithful to complete it" (author's translation and emphasis). This translation accurately picks up both the promise of God and the place of our transformation. The promise is that God is at work in each of us and in all of us. The place is the Christian community (hence the phrase "among you"), in which God is actively and powerfully present. Biblically, virtue is not the attainment of a solo saint striving to be good but a by-product of a virtuous community in which all seek to live out their Christian convictions in the real world.

What this means to you and me is that while we start this process of living commendably by trusting God in faith, we also learn to live each day in prayerful dependence on God's guidance and transforming work in our lives in companionship with other believers. If we truly want our faith to speak to others, we not only must have genuine faith but also must live as part of a community of faith that supports us, exhorts us, and encourages us to demonstrate the grace of God in our lives every day in the real world.

As I bring this chapter to a close, I want to speak to those of you who feel as if you have stumbled on the very first step. It is frustrating to feel as if you have gotten off on the wrong foot. If you are discouraged, remember that you are in good company. All of us, including well-known teachers of virtue and pastors who write books on 2 Peter, have come up short when our lives are measured by the goodness of God. And to make matters worse, the very times when we are compromising our convictions the most are also the times when we are the most tempted to try to pull ourselves out of our problems by our own efforts, thus slipping even farther away from biblical righteousness. It can become a terrible downward spiral.

This is, of course, very disappointing and deeply painful. But let us not forget that all it takes to be restored to God is to turn back and trust him again. By admitting our failures, by abandoning our self-righteousness, and by acknowledging our need for God's grace and mercy, we climb back onto the gondola of faith. And faith alone leads to genuine, godly virtue—the first real step toward becoming a person whose very life speaks to the world of the redeeming, reconciling power of the gospel of Jesus Christ.

Questions to Consider

1. Think of someone whom you would call a good person. Now describe them without using the word *good*. How do you feel about this person? How do you feel when you are around this person?
2. In every ancient list, the most important terms are the first and the last. Since Peter's list of char-

acter qualities begins with *faith* and ends with *love*, what can we infer about the qualities listed in between?

3. We stated that the Greek word for goodness in this text is a more classical or "secular" term. Why do you think this might be important? What is the point we want to impress upon believers?

4. We learned that God's power and God's promises are the resources we have for producing goodness from our faith. If goodness is living commendably to nonbelievers because of faith, then what do you need to do to access God's power and rely on his promises?

5. What does it mean to you to live dependently on God in order to produce virtue? What do you need God to do in your life? What specific change do you need to make in your living? Ask God to produce virtue in your life, and commit yourself to do anything that the Spirit and the Scriptures instruct you to do to live virtuously.

3 IT'S NOT WHAT YOU KNOW

For this very reason, you must make every effort to support your faith with goodness, and goodness with knowledge.

NRSV

From your virtue, produce a wisdom that can apply that virtue in real-world situations.

author's translation

Know What?

Recently I read of a seventeen-year-old high school senior in Fremont, California, who made national news in 1996 when she did something truly remarkable. She achieved a perfect 800 score on both sections of the Scholastic Aptitude Test and a perfect 8,000 on the tough University of California acceptance index. Never in history had a student accomplished this feat. At her high school, she was known as Wonder Woman because of her brains. She went on to Harvard the following fall. But what was interesting in the news story was a little exchange between her and a reporter. He asked, "What is the meaning of life?" She replied, "I have no idea."[1]

Now, this shouldn't be a surprise to us, and I certainly don't want to be critical of this remarkable young woman, but we all know that being smart is not the same thing as being wise. And knowledge is a lot more than information.

In this chapter, we will take the next step for living out the gospel in the real world. Having learned to produce from our faith virtue, now we seek to develop from virtue knowledge.

It is interesting to note that in the secular character lists of the first century, knowledge was usually listed first or last, meaning that it was considered either the fundamental requirement for living well or the highest aspiration. But in most Christian lists, knowledge is displaced by faith and love. The desire to know, to master, to be enlightened, to have insight is not abandoned but instead is made subservient to the true goal of living out one's faith in an effective and fruitful way. It's not what you know that counts but how you use what you know as an expression of your faith in Christ.

This is even more evident when we recognize that the Greek word for knowledge here in 2 Peter 1, *gnosis*, is not the word for the basic saving knowledge of God in Christ, which makes a person a Christian. When 2 Peter wants to indicate saving knowledge, the author instead uses a different Greek word, *epignosis*. *Gnosis* is best understood as "the wisdom and discernment which the Christian needs for a virtuous life and which is progressively acquired."[2]

In other words, Peter is not telling us that we need to learn more information and get smarter. Nor is he encouraging us to find secret keys to living well. Instead, he is telling us that our virtue needs to be applied wisely in real-life situations. The next step for following Christ into the world with lives that proclaim the Good News is applying wisdom to virtue in real-world situations.

TMI: Too Much Information

When the teenagers in my church want to tell someone that they are taking too long to tell a story or are revealing embarrassing or trivial information, they will say, "Hey bud, TMI." Too much information. It is a cryptic way of saying, "Don't say anything more; I can't handle what you've told me already." Well, today we live in a TMI world.

We live in a world that wants to sell us plenty of unnecessary information and seeks to play on our emotions and insecurities. We are told that the knowledge we need to succeed in a complex world is found only by buying tapes from an infomercial guru or enrolling in the best schools or reading the latest expert.

Peter is telling us that the secret of living out an effective faith is not in new gimmicks, new books, or new information but in applying ancient and enduring knowledge to the world today.

Italian violinists of the seventeenth century were known to keep toads in their violin cases to improve their performances. Just before a concert, the musicians would pull out their toads and stroke them for good luck. They believed that the amphibians would keep their hands from perspiring.

Seems strange, doesn't it? Know any violinists today who keep toads in their cases? Sheer superstition and folklore, right? Well, recently it was discovered that the folk wisdom of these debunked baroque ancestors may

51

not have been far off the mark. According to herpetologists, most species of toads secrete an alkaloid substance that tends to dry out human skin. That's why small cuts can be painful to those who play with toads. It's like dabbing your wounds with alcohol. While the toads likely did not give violinists good luck, they might well have kept them from getting sweaty palms.

If you want a really good solution to an everyday problem, you should not ignore ancient wisdom just because it is old.

Another ancient teacher, St. Augustine, once said, "Man wishes to be happy even when he so lives as to make happiness impossible." According to Augustine, the big problem with finding happiness, and this is as true today as it was in the fifth century, is that people refuse to believe that the greatest hindrances to our happiness are the foolish choices we make. Augustine was part of a great line of ethical teachers who believed that if we want to be truly happy, we must choose the good.

Choosing Wisely and Well

How do you make the decisions of your life? Especially the important ones, the decisions that determine your direction and maybe your destiny. When a road forks in a wood, how do you decide which direction to travel?

Of course, lots of decisions are relatively inconsequential. I hope you didn't spend too much time praying about what clothes to wear this morning or what kind of muffin to have with your coffee. But some decisions—even seemingly small ones—will contribute to or deduct from your experience of the good life more than anything else.

The summer before my freshman year in college, I went to a training retreat for those who wanted to join Youth for Christ's Campus Life high school ministry. I would be moving to the San Fernando Valley in a few weeks, and I went to the retreat to interview with the leaders of that chapter and to prepare for my move. Working with the chapter was going to be my first ministry position.

One night a group of us decided that we'd all go watch the movie *Poltergeist*, which was brand new then and really scary, and then play hide-and-seek in a nearby graveyard. It seemed like a relatively harmless bit of adolescent mischief. But as we were getting ready to go, I caught the eye of one of the senior staff members for the Valley Campus Life team and saw her shake her head. I decided to pull out and let the others go on ahead.

Two hours later, the group came back after having been caught by police for trespassing. My soon-to-be boss at Valley Campus Life was a former Los Angeles police officer who felt very strongly that Christian youth leaders should obey the law if they are going to represent Christ to teenagers. He told me later that if I had gone on that little excursion, he would not have hired me, that it would have indicated to him that I lacked character and discernment. That seemingly small decision could have drastically changed my life, and how close I came to making a bad one only revealed how much I needed to continue to develop biblical wisdom in my life.

However, an important but often misunderstood principle is that the Bible does not lay out a map for every decision. God cares more about our character in making choices than about the number of good choices we make. Famous missionary E. Stanley Jones once wrote, "God must guide in a way that will develop spontaneity in us. The development of character, rather than direction in this, that and the other matter, must be the primary purpose of the Father. He will guide us, but he will not override us."

That being the case, when we look to the Bible, we should be looking for *guidance* for making good decisions, guidance that, during the decision-making process, helps us increase in wisdom. Certainly the Bible gives us a framework for making most important decisions, particularly moral decisions, decisions that shape our soul and set our paths. Some are obvious: the decision to follow Christ, the decision to obey the law even when others flaunt it, the choice of a mate, the selection of the values you'll teach your children, the commitments of your heart. Others may be less obvious but no less important: Whom do I choose as friends? How do I break up with a love? What business practices do I use? How do I fire an employee or treat a customer? How do I care for aging parents? What medical treatment do I choose for myself? How do I spend my money?

But in the Bible, wisdom is less about making a particular decision than it is about a disposition. Wisdom is the reflection of a character developed through the habit of morally wise decision-making. This is demonstrated profoundly in Proverbs 3. The opening stanza has two sections of two couplets each:

> My child, do not forget my teaching, but let your heart
>   keep my commandments;
>   for length of days and years of life and abundant
>   welfare they will give you.
> Do not let loyalty and faithfulness forsake you; bind
>   them around your neck,
>   write them on the tablet of your heart.
> So you will find favor and good repute in the sight of
>   God and of people.

verses 1–4 NRSV

Here, and in the following stanza (vv. 5–8), we see two principles joined for building the habit of wise decision-making: the Word and the community, both an obligation to obey God and the commitment to make decisions for the good of the people of God.

Let me warn you to avoid the trap of trying to separate one from the other or to pit one against the other. Wise decisions demand both. So when you are making a decision, I urge you to ask two questions:

- Is what I want to do consistent with the Word of God?
- Does it contribute to the well-being of the community of God's people?

So that we'll really understand this, let's separate them for a minute and look at each of them.

What's the Word Say?

Proverbs 3:1 tells us, "My child, do not forget my teaching, but let your heart keep my commandments" (NRSV).

The first place to look if we want to make wise decisions is always the Scriptures. First things first: Does the Bible speak clearly about this? Is there a clear command to obey, a clear word to follow? Very often, we talk about difficult decisions when we should be talking about hard decisions. Difficult decisions are those for which we don't have clear guidance. Hard decisions are those for which the guidance is clear but the correct choice is not our preference.

A man came to see me who was interested in starting a relationship with a coworker, and he wanted me to help him sort out the biblical perspective on this kind of romantic entanglement. He was fretting over the decision, very confused and unsure. An office romance could be problematic, and this was a difficult decision. I listened to him for a while and then pointed out that while the Bible doesn't seem to address some decisions directly, in this case it did. You see, he had told me almost in passing that he had a wife and three kids. And the Bible is very clear that a man with a wife and three kids should not start another romantic relationship, whether it is with a coworker or not!

This was a *hard* decision for the man: his marriage was not fulfilling, he was falling in love with the coworker, his emotions were in an upheaval. But it wasn't very difficult. It was actually quite clear what he was to do.

Recently I was talking to a pastor friend about a decision I needed to make. I spoke for ten minutes about how tricky the decision was, how easily it could be misinterpreted by others, how even some people in my church might think ill of me.

Finally, my friend said, "Well, those things are hard, but are you at all confused about what the right thing to do is?"

"No," I said.

"Then do that," he replied.

The wisdom that leads to steady steps blessed by God, according to St. Augustine, is "the soul oriented to eternal things." It is the realigning of ourselves so that we live each day cleaving to the truth of God. As Proverbs 10:8 says, "The wise of heart will heed commandments" (NRSV).

Now, this is easier said than done. Sometimes even the decision to heed God's commands is a really hard one. Peer pressure doesn't end when we leave behind our high school locker rooms; it is just as prevalent in company boardrooms. Temptations to cheat, cut corners, exaggerate the truth, break our vows, or use our influence to unfairly get ahead abound. I really do understand this. I face these temptations every day, and probably once a week I talk to someone who is facing a hard decision between right and wrong. What I have found is that when we talk together, we rarely have to figure out the right course of action. What we most need is an encourager, an accountability partner, and a friend who will pray for us to go through with what is right.

Virtue that produces wisdom heeds the Word of God in every circumstance, clinging to the truth of God and trusting that it is the surest path to blessedness. And sometimes we just need others to help us remember that and to support us as we make the hard decision to act wisely.

But what do we do when Scripture doesn't offer explicit commands? Is this when we trust our gut? Listen to our hearts? Let our conscience be our guide? Well, yes and no. You see, even when the Bible doesn't command with a "thou shalt not," it usually offers principles with which we can make good decisions.

In a world that is influenced more by Jimminy Cricket than by Jesus Christ and tells us to go with our gut or follow our hearts, we should pause to hear Proverbs 3:5–6: "Trust in the LORD with all your heart, and do not rely on your own insight. In all your ways acknowledge him, and he will make straight your paths" (NRSV).

Let me suggest that if your mind is not filled with the Scriptures and your heart is not in the habit of obeying them, then to trust your gut or go with your own insight is to walk a crooked and perilous path. But if you fill your mind and your heart with Scripture, you can probably trust your gut.

Do you know enough Scripture to confidently base your decisions on it? Perhaps the first step toward making blessed decisions is just learning more of the Bible. It is to commit ourselves to read Scripture regularly and join an in-depth study. I know that some of us find the Bible hard to read on our own. That is why at our church we encourage everyone to be in a small group in which the Bible is studied and in which together we can learn, grow in understanding, and have others help us answer this first decision-making question: is that which I want to do consistent with the Word of God?

Of course, being in a small-group Bible study also helps us with the second criterion for wise decisions.

What's Good for God's People?

Picture yourself living out your faith in the real world. You have experienced the gracious power of God saving you. You have determined to live a life of following Christ that makes a difference to your friends and colleagues. You have begun to take steps of virtue, and now you have reached a fork in the path. You have a key decision to make. You are uncertain which way to go. What do you do?

If you are like most people, you say, "Just make a decision and do my best." Or you might say, "See what the Bible says, and then make a decision and do my best."

But let me ask you to consider this: is there anybody there with you at the fork in the path? When you pictured yourself, did you assume you were alone? If you are like most people, the answer is, "Of course. You didn't say that there was anyone else. I thought this was a journey of character. Isn't that an individual pursuit?"

You're right. I didn't mention there being anyone with you. But I also didn't say that you were alone. Second Peter says "you," but why did you assume that it was a singular *you*? In fact, it is plural.

58

Let me push you a bit. Why did you assume that when you rode the gondola of faith, you were the only one being taken out of the corruption of the world? The truth, of course, is that the gondola is as big as God himself and saves everyone who calls on the name of the Lord. It is the gondola of the communion of saints, as the old creeds would put it, and it is filled with the great cloud of witnesses (Heb. 12:1) and God's own people (1 Peter 2:10).

My friends, the next step is learning to do what is best for all of God's people and not just yourself. We will talk more later about the importance of church and love for our brothers and sisters, but even here in the early going, we learn that the key to growing in the knowledge that applies goodness to real-world situations is both to apply the Word and to seek the welfare of the community of believers.

Notice that in both stanzas at the beginning of Proverbs 3, a couplet about the Word is followed by a couplet about relating to the people of God:

- "My child, do not forget my teaching, but let your heart keep my commandments" is joined to "Do not let loyalty and faithfulness forsake you; bind them around your neck, write them on the tablet of your heart."
- "Trust in the LORD with all your heart, and do not rely on your own insight" is joined to "Do not be wise in your own eyes; fear the LORD, and turn away from evil."

And both of these couplets end with the promise of blessing. If we join obedience to the Word to faithfulness to each other, and trusting the Lord to seeking wisdom from others, then we are promised that

- "length of days and years of life and abundant welfare they will give you" (v. 2).
- "you will find favor and good repute in the sight of God and of people" (v. 4).
- "it will be a healing for your flesh and a refreshment for your body" (v. 8).

If we want to figure out how to make virtue apply to real-life situations, we must not only listen to the word of Scripture but also consider the impact on the community. In every decision, we shouldn't just ask, Is this right for me? We should also ask, Is this right for us? How will this affect us? Will this decision make a negative impact on the church? And, even better, Will it contribute to the well-being of my brothers and sisters in Christ?

As a pastor, the most heart-rending decisions I have had to make are those when I knew that for the good of the community, I had to go against the wishes of one person or even my own desires. I have had to ask elders to resign whose lives were morally compromised and whose lack of credibility would hurt our ministry. I have had to ask people to leave a church or withdraw from a small group when they were causing division and pain. I have had to make difficult personnel decisions when someone's inability was hindering the work of Christ.

Making hard decisions like these goes against the grain for most of us. But it's a core issue. If we traced our unhappiness and missteps to a single cause, this would be the one: we want to be good people, but we want to be good people on our own.

We don't want to consider how our decisions impact others. And we certainly don't want others' opinions, advice, or counsel. We want to trust our own minds, our own hearts, our own insight. We want to solve our own problems and take care of our own dilemmas. Proverbs 12:15 says, "Fools think their own way is right, but the wise listen to advice" (NRSV).

By far the most important decisions of my life were the decisions to marry Beth and to come to San Clemente Presbyterian Church as their pastor. In both of these decisions, not only did I search the Scriptures but I also submitted my decision to small groups of friends who prayed with me, asked searching questions, and even challenged the idea. Beth and I were young when we got married, and we didn't exactly come out of the best family backgrounds. We needed all the help and counsel we could get. Becoming a senior pastor at thirty-three was a huge step, and there was some concern about my being up to the task. Further, my coming to San Clemente meant leaving friends and a ministry that had been very important to me. It was painful indeed. But the blessings of being married to Beth and being the pastor of my church have been, along with our children, the greatest of my life. It is not insignificant to me that in both situations, I didn't make a decision until the community of Christians around me gave its blessing.

Conclusion: Valuable Lessons Drenched in Pain

General Simon Bolivar Buckner of the Confederate Army liked to tell the story of an old resident in his Kentucky home who was celebrated for his down-home wisdom.

"Uncle Zeke," a young man once asked this man, "how does it come you're so wise?"

"Because," said the old man, "I've got good judgment."

"So," the young man asked, "how do you get good judgment?"

61

"Good judgment comes from experience," he replied, "and experience, well, that comes from poor judgment." Someone once said that every proverb is the pain-drenched wisdom of many and the wit of one. The great temptation for many of us is to barrel down the mountain by ourselves, hoping for the best. But we have these teachings given to us today as lessons learned through others' poor judgment. The only question is, Will we learn from it? In our world today, basing decisions on the Word and on the community may seem like keeping a toad in a violin case. But this ancient wisdom is still true today.

Is it consistent with the Word of God? Does it contribute to the well-being of the community? If we can learn to make decisions by asking these two questions, we will be that much closer to living a life that preaches the gospel in the real world before we have ever said a word.

Questions to Consider

1. Who is the wisest person you know? What other words would you use to describe him or her?
2. Biblical teaching holds that all true blessedness or happiness depends on holiness. How do you understand this connection? Read Proverbs 3:13–18, 21–26. Why is wisdom necessary for happiness?
3. The first criterion for making wise choices is consistency with the Word of God. What do you need in order to help you make choices consistent with the Word of God?
4. The second criterion is whether a decision contributes to the well-being of the community of God's people. How could you apply this in seemingly private or personal decisions?

5. Which is more difficult for you: knowing what God's Word says about a decision, or considering the interests and well-being of the community? Why is that?
6. What decision do you need to reconsider in light of these criteria?

4 TO BE A MIGHTY RIVER

For this very reason, you must make every effort to support your faith with goodness, and goodness with knowledge, and knowledge with self-control.

NRSV

From your wisdom, produce a self-control that can enjoy freedom in Christ while knowing safe limits.

author's translation

The Cost of Choosing Poorly

Would you rather be a river or a swamp? On the surface, that's an easy question. Rivers, after all, are rushing and majestic; swamps are stagnant and rancid. Rivers are filled with trout and salmon; swamps with snakes and crocodiles. People picnic by rivers, swim in rivers, fish in rivers, build homes and entire cities by rivers. People avoid swamps.

It seems simple, doesn't it? We all would rather be rivers, and in fact we are attracted to and mesmerized by them. So it is curious that we usually choose to be swamps—at great cost to our lives and often to the lives of others.

Why is this so? Why, if we could choose to be a mighty river, would we ever settle for being merely a swamp?

I think it's because we don't properly understand or acknowledge the difference between a river and a swamp. What makes a river mighty is its banks, its limits, its boundaries. Only with a solid bottom and firm sides does a river become a rushing, clear, beautiful, life-producing, life-sustaining waterway upon the banks of which whole civilizations are built. Yet most of us don't want to be limited. Something within us balks at the idea of limits, commandments, control, and boundaries.

But after we have taken the first step of using faith to produce goodness or virtue, and the second step of using goodness to produce knowledge or wisdom, we are called to use knowledge to produce self-control. And, believe it or not, this is one of the very best qualities we have to offer the world.

A Surprising Secret of Success

In 1992, psychologist David G. Myers wrote a book called *The Pursuit of Happiness: Who Is Happy and Why?* It is a study of how Americans are doing in the pursuit of happiness, our favorite inalienable right from the Declaration of Independence. Myers reveals that between 1957 and 1990, the per capita income in America doubled in real terms. At the same time, however, the number of people who reported being "very happy" did not change one bit. In 1990, still only about a third of Americans said they were very happy. Having more, experiencing more, and living with more didn't make us any happier. In fact, Myers concludes the opposite is the case: the happiest people are those who intentionally limit themselves.

Myers writes, "Well-being is found in the renewal of disciplined lifestyles, committed relationships and the giving and receiving of acceptance. To experience deep well-being is to be self-confident yet self-conscious, self-giving yet self-respecting, realistic yet hope-filled."[1]

Think about that. Happiness comes from disciplined lifestyles, committed relationships, and an affirming but limited role for the self.

Myers's findings should come as no surprise. In the seventeenth century, British writer Thomas Fuller wrote that "riches enlarge, rather than satisfy, appetites." And Henry David Thoreau would later observe, "A man is rich in proportion to the things he can afford to let alone."

In this chapter, we will learn that the next step for following Jesus into the real world is a self-limiting step. We will learn that one of the keys to an effective and fruitful life that speaks to others is developing the ability to live within limits for the sake of love. It is developing the strength of self to enjoy freedom in Christ without threatening your effective living. It is developing what could be termed "bolstered boundaries," what classically has been called "temperance," what the Bible refers to as "self-control."

Tempting Temperance

The concept of *temperance*, that often misunderstood and misused term, can actually be quite attractive when it's properly understood. Temperance is not about squelching pleasure; it is about affirming that pleasure for which we were created. Temperance affirms pleasure as something

God gave us to be enjoyed in freedom for his glory and our good. But in order for pleasure to be for God's glory and our good, it must be enjoyed within boundaries.

Once I met with a couple that asked me to perform their wedding. With deep love in their eyes, they told me that all they wanted was to live openly and freely without limits, so that nothing could keep them from experiencing total happiness with each other. I asked them, "You're saying you want your marriage to have no limits?" The man quickly said, "Yes!" but the woman paused an instant and said, "No!" For limits are exactly why we take vows, aren't they? Without vows, marriage is nothing more than an adolescent romance in which couples flit in and out of commitment—swampy living par excellence.

One of the key points that Peter makes is this: faith that produces character and speaks in the real world willingly lives within limits for the sake of love. In a world in which so many people live, and even flaunt, lives that are out of control, biblical self-control results in an attractive life that is both good and safe, pleasurable and beneficial.

If you are attracted to the beauty of the rushing river of self-control, you are likely to ask a very practical question: How? How do we produce godly self-control?

Allow me to suggest three action steps:

1. Know yourself.
2. Control only yourself.
3. Make love your aim, not control.

1. Know Yourself

I spent my early years in ministry with young adults, both college students and young graduates, who were entering their first jobs and careers, experiencing their first serious relationships, and using their first credit cards. Over and over, I saw people abuse their new freedoms. Oh, some of it was immaturity, but often patterns were repeated again and again. I was often confused by the fact that so many people seemed eager to live out-of-control lives. Taking on debts, rushing headlong into one relationship after another, abusing alcohol and drugs, indulging in one fad after another. My wife, a marriage and family therapist, often reminded me that people don't act self-destructively without good reason, though they may not know what it is or be able to admit it. In truth, usually the teenager who is rebelling, the young adult who is spending the limit on the credit card, the husband who is raging out of control, and the wife who can't keep her vow would prefer not to act in these ways. But the unresolved issues in their lives often drive them to overrun the limits of life like a car hurtling through a stop sign.

What I have learned in the ministry is affirmed by the great teachers: where there is no deep sense of self, there is no self-control. The beginning of godly self-control is an honest self-appraisal that begins by asking, How well do I live within limits for the sake of love? How developed are my boundaries? How firm are the banks containing my living?

For some of us, this might mean taking a sober self-inventory and acknowledging the places in our lives that are out of control. We may need the help of friends or professionals, or an accountability or support group, to help us develop the inner strength to live within healthy limits. Perhaps the most healthy, holy, and honest response is acknowledging that we lack self-control and that we need the assistance of God and others.

But there is perhaps an even more important point. One of the reasons why so many of us struggle with producing genuinely Christ-centered self-control is that, no matter what stage of life we're in, we still don't have an honest and accurate sense of self. We really don't know who we are. We struggle with various roles that we feel we are forced to play, with the inner voices that torment us, with the expectations of others. Whether it is a four-year-old developing a childhood self, a fourteen-year-old trying to master an adolescent self, or a forty-year-old in a midlife crisis trying to find a "real self," the absence of a strong, biblically rooted self-definition leads us to let our confused desires overflow the boundaries of our lives.

In the introduction to his famous *Institutes of the Christian Religion*, John Calvin writes that all wisdom for living is directly dependent on the knowledge of God and the knowledge of self. For Calvin, both are so closely related that "like rivulets that lead to the same stream," they will eventually flow together.[2] Calvin would tell us that self-knowledge is impossible unless we know ourselves from God's perspective.

Only as we understand that God knows us and loves us do we develop accurate self-knowledge. Do you want to hear how the God who really knows you feels about you? Listen to just one description from Isaiah: "Can a woman forget her nursing child, or show no compassion for the child of her womb? Even these may forget, yet I will not forget you. See, I have inscribed you on the palms of my hands" (49:15–16 NRSV).

Can a woman forget her child? Can a father abandon his children? As quickly as we who are parents would shout our denial, we know that all too often that is exactly what happens. Our television newscasts are filled with tragic stories of parents harming their children. Whether it is the young woman who drowned her children in a bathtub or the young father-to-be who was accused of killing his pregnant wife and unborn son, we are painfully aware that even the parent-child bond can be broken all too easily. It is heart-wrenching when it happens, and something within us wells up in vehement protest because we know that it shouldn't happen. But it does.

Not with God.

"Even if mothers and fathers forget their children, I will never forget you," God says to you. He knows everything about you and never takes his eye off you. The Bible tells you that God has numbered every hair on your head, knows every sparrow that falls, and has called you to follow him. God even says that he has engraved your name on the palms of his hands. Whenever you consider the nail-scarred hands of Jesus, see not only his brutal wounds but also your name etched in the scars, your name held before him.

This is how the God who really knows you feels about you. The first step toward self-control is knowing yourself as God sees you.

2. Control Only Yourself

When we are feeling out of control, one of the most tempting things to do is to focus on everyone and everything other than ourselves. So we obsess about keeping a clean house. We rage at our spouses when really it is our emotions that are out of control. We nag our kids to be perfect. We struggle with eating disorders. We try to control every minute of the day and yet have no inner peace.

If self-control is limiting ourselves for the sake of love, then we must resist our attempts to control other people and everything around us. Self-control demands that we acknowledge that only God is in control of everything.

In the middle of our church's first building campaign, I went through a patch filled with anxiety. I slept in fits and starts and obsessed over details. I tried to control everything down to the last comma and fretted over whether people would support the plan. I knew God had called us to follow this plan, and I was convinced it was the right time, but there was no way I could control what people thought or did.

It was beginning to drive me crazy, and others close to me could tell. And at just the right time, an anonymous angel sent me a framed card that read, "Tod, trust me. I have everything under control. Love, Jesus."

I sat in my office smiling at this card. Once I began to trust God with the details and the results of the campaign, I was much freer to focus on what God wanted to do in me. This was not a job just for me, the pastor; it was a call to my family and me as Christians. Once I acknowledged what was beyond my control, I could embrace the challenge that was genuinely within my control. Beth and I began to pray more specifically about our giving sacrificially to this building project. We focused not on all the details of the campaign but on being as personally committed to the campaign as I was calling others to be. In the end, Beth and I made the biggest financial commitment to the ministry of Christ that we have ever made, and that was by far the most life-changing part of the campaign for me.

3. Make Love Your Aim, Not Control

In the first century, a group of teachers called the Stoics tried to convince people that the only way to truly be free was to live in accordance with reason and to avoid letting emotion or passion influence their thinking. They taught that the key to self-control was being rational and logical.

While this may be an attractive ideology, most of us know that logical reasons do not usually provide enough motivation to make a change. You can hear all the information in the world about why you should lower your cholesterol, but until something touches your soul, you'll probably never make the appointment to get your heart checked.

On this point, the Bible and Christian teaching are consistent: only love motivates us to change. Love of life, love of family, love of Christ. If we want to be people of genuine, godly self-control, we must make love our aim, and not control.

The Stoics said that you can control yourself with reason; Christianity replaced reason with love. Love is the highest aim; not freedom, not knowledge, not even virtue, just love. Famous missionary E. Stanley Jones said, "The love of Christ constrains me." Another way to say it is, "Because of the love of Christ, I live within limits."

The word *self-control* is especially relevant to us in our culture of sexual permissiveness. In a world in which the vast majority of media images and references are to sexual experiences outside of marriage, it is important to note that in this passage, the word used for self-control most often refers to refraining from sexual immorality and living within the limits of biblical sexual ethics—something all of us find difficult to do at some point in our lives.

My wife, Beth, and I met when we were in our late teens, and we dated in college. Like most people, the deeper I felt for Beth, the closer I wanted to be to her. After five years of dating, the temptation to compromise our convictions was pretty strong. I was beginning to find it difficult to practice the kind of self-control referred to in this passage.

Around this time Beth and I went on a retreat that our church sponsored for college students. The topic was Christian sexuality, and once again we were reminded that God intends sexual expression for marriage. I knew all the information that was being taught; as a volunteer youth worker, I had even taught it to younger teenagers. But near the end of the retreat, the pastor asked us each to consider this question: "If Jesus were here, what would he say to you about your sexuality? What would he say to you about your relationship?" At that moment, it was almost like Jesus was standing there in front of me. I knew clear well what he would say. He would remind me how much he loves Beth. He would remind me that he loves her deeply, that her name is etched on his palms, that he died on the cross for her sins, that he had numbered every hair on her head, that he had seen every tear fall from her eyes, and that he knew every hope in her heart. He would remind me that he loved her sacrificially, honestly, without manipulation, without impurity. And in the quietness of my heart, he asked me, "Will you love her any less?"

It was because of our love for Christ and for each other that we, through many frustrating evenings and many cold showers, lived within the limits of being obedient to Christ in this most intimate arena of our lives. Trying to replicate Christ's love for my wife remains my constant motivation.

A significant reason why 2 Peter 1:3–8 means so much to me today is that it was the passage I chose to have read at our wedding—not the famous love passage of 1 Corinthians, not the romantic passages of Song of Songs, but this list of character qualities. Maybe it was because we both came from broken homes. Maybe it was because we were a bit overwhelmed with getting married in our early twenties. Maybe it was because I knew full well the weakness of my flesh. But I knew that if this marriage was going to work, our faith needed to produce character. Love motivates us to character, and through character comes the self-control we need to protect our love.

Conclusion: Enjoying Real Pleasure While Avoiding Cliffs and Edges

I want to stress one final thought: it is tempting when hearing a message on self-control to think, *Well, here's another Christian trying to take all the pleasure out of life.* Hear me on this. We are not ascetics. There is no goodness in limitations or self-sacrifice for their own sakes. We don't turn down worldly pleasures just because they are pleasurable. Indeed, we enjoy everything as a gift from God. The Scripture's commands are not to keep us from pleasure but to protect us from the excesses of pleasure, and this leads us *to* pleasure.

My favorite wintertime activity is skiing. Those of you who ski know that the key to having fun is the ability to exercise two skills that, ironically, are ways of staying within boundaries or limits: turning and stopping. If you can't turn or stop, you will fly out of control and hurt yourself or someone else. Instead of skiing, you fall. And sit. And hurt. But once you can confidently turn and stop, you are free to go as fast and have as much fun as you can.

Self-control is learning how to turn your life away from cliffs and edges, to stop your momentum when the good pleasures of life head out of bounds, to experience the confident freedom of a skier on a pristine powdery slope.

Real-world faith lives with limitations for the sake of love and produces self-control, which comes from knowing yourself, controlling only yourself, and making love your aim.

Whenever we talk about self-control, our minds usually wander to one particular area of our lives, one particular place where we feel most out of control, where our faith seems painfully ineffective and unfruitful. It may be a struggle with daily discipline like balancing your life, cultivating better health, or having regular times of prayer. It may be an emotional struggle like gaining control over anger, negative self-talk, or anxiety. It may be an addiction to alcohol, drugs, gambling, sex, or pornography. It may be relatively harmless day to day, or it may be devastating to your life, but it is in this place that you feel your faith is useless.

What can we do? For starters, we can do the things we have talked about in this chapter. But this is exactly where the idea of a community of character comes in. The more stuck we are, the more we need to turn to the power and promises of God made real to us through caring and wise Christians. We need others to share the struggle with us. We need pastors and counselors and friends to pray for us, challenge us, and remind us that God is the one who is changing us.

If you find yourself dwelling on one particularly problematic area, let me challenge you not to let the sun go down without asking someone you trust to pray about this with you. Find someone and ask him or her to help you to trust the promises and power of God to bring you self-control—and as a consequence, real freedom—in this area of your life.

God's power has given us all we need for life and godliness. If we trust and focus on the love of Christ, our faith will become more effective. So together, let our faith produce goodness, let goodness produce knowledge, and let knowledge produce self-control. And as he works in us together, our faith will rush forward into the world like a mighty river.

Questions to Consider

1. When you think of boundaries, limits, and constraints, what connotations come to mind? How about self-control? Are your responses to these two words different?
2. Reread the paraphrase of the biblical text for this chapter. What are your reactions? Why do you think there is a progression from faith to love? How is self-control dependent on wisdom?
3. If you were to explain the value of self-control to a rock musician who has unlimited money and opportunities for pleasure and has virtually no accountability, what would you say?
4. Respond to St. Augustine's statement: "Love God and do whatever you want." Is this good advice? What do you think he meant?
5. Reread the main points for developing godly self-control. What is the most difficult step for you? Why? What do you need from God or Christian friends?

5 BEING AN EVERYDAY HERO

For this very reason, you must make every effort to support your faith with goodness, and goodness with knowledge, and knowledge with self-control, and self-control with endurance.

NRSV

From that inner strength, produce endurance to face whatever challenge arises before you.

author's translation

A Surprising Standing O

In the summer of 2001, my family went with some friends to see an Anaheim Angels game at Edison Field in Anaheim, California. It was a low-scoring ball game, a pitchers' duel. The sun was blazing and a number of people headed home early. It was the kind of game that only hardcore baseball fans like us could enjoy, sitting in cheap outfield seats.

The Angels were losing to the Baltimore Orioles, 1-0, when the Orioles came up to bat in the top of the ninth inning. The first batter reached second base. The tension was mounting; a base hit would add to the Orioles' lead. Into the batter's box stepped their All-Star third baseman. And then the oddest thing happened. Every person at Edison Field—all the hardcore, committed, vocal Angels fans—stood and gave a rousing ovation to the opposing team's player. It didn't matter that this man could single-handedly destroy any chance of an Angel comeback. It didn't matter that the game was on the line. At that moment, the game took a backseat to the man, for that Oriole was Cal Ripken Jr., and this was the last time he would ever bat at Edison Field.

If you're not a baseball fan, you should know that Cal Ripken Jr. is a sure, unanimous, first-ballot Hall of Famer. He is a great player who had a great career. He hit over four hundred home runs and over three thousand hits, and he led his team to a World Series victory in 1983. But the reason Cal Ripken Jr. received a standing ovation from opposing fans all over the country is because he set a most extraordinary record for doing the most ordinary thing. For over fifteen years, he never missed a day of work. Between 1982 and 1998, he didn't miss a single game, playing in 2,632 consecutively and breaking by over five hundred the record previously held by Yankee great Lou Gehrig.

In a world where sticking with something is rare, be it a marriage, a job, or a promise, perhaps Ripken is just the kind of hero we are looking for.

Similarly, in the aftermath of the terrorist strikes of September 11, 2001, thousands of ordinary members of fire departments and police departments were hailed as national heroes, not merely because they served us during that one moment in history but because they had been there for us in both ordinary and extraordinary times.

In this chapter, we will learn that living out biblical faith involves the simple but essential act of reporting for duty every single day. Being a Sunday Christian won't cut it. Faith for the real world must endure outside of church.

Our next step is to learn that "effective faith for the real world," faith that is fruitful and makes a difference, is faith that endures. And the character attributes produced by faith—goodness, knowledge, and self-control—must be consistently and dependably expressed. Faith that works is expressed in both character and constancy.

What is endurance, really? It's the indefatigable, steady, step-by-step, face-into-the-wind striving to stay on course for the long run. Christian endurance is comprised of two elements: showing up every day and putting up with everyday annoyances.

Showing Up Every Day

Twenty years ago, Eugene Peterson wrote some words that are even more appropriate today:

We assume that if something can be done at all, it can be done quickly and efficiently. Our attention spans have been conditioned by thirty-second commercials. . . . It is not difficult in such a world to get a person interested in the message of the gospel; it is terrifically difficult to sustain the interest. . . . Many claim to have been born again, but the evidence for mature Christian discipleship is slim. . . . There is a great market for religious experience in our world; there is little enthusiasm for the patient acquisition of virtue, little inclination to sign up for a long apprenticeship in what earlier generations of Christians called holiness.[1]

Peterson titled his book *A Long Obedience in the Same Direction*, which comes from a quote from Friedrich Nietzsche about what makes life worth living. Even the most excited Christians often balk at the long apprenticeship of applying faith to virtue day after day. But that is what endurance is in 2 Peter. It is not just flash-in-the-pan faithfulness once in a while. It is not Christmas and Easter attendance, every-now-and-then prayer, self-control on occasion. Endurance is about showing up for Christ and faithfully and consistently exhibiting virtue, wisdom, and self-control. Not perfectly, but on a trajectory of constancy.

Peterson is still right. Two decades of hyperactive, microwave-ready, two-inch-deep living has left the world yearning for people of enduring faithfulness. The world is looking for heroes who endure. Our endurance testifies to a faith that makes a difference every day and offers something attractive to the world around us.

In the 1972 Munich Olympics, Dave Wottle set the world on fire with an 800-meter race for the ages. Wearing his trademark baseball cap, Wottle started the gold-medal race in the back of the field, dead last. As the final lap around the track began, Wottle charged through the pack. The television announcer screamed into the microphone, "Watch out for the kick of Dave Wottle!" Wottle overtook the leaders in the last twenty meters and won the gold medal by three-tenths of a second. An amazing, stunning kick.

Wottle became a symbol for a typically mythic American value: the great comeback. Many Americans think, *That's exciting—that's how I want to run. It doesn't matter if I fall behind; I'll make it back with a big kick as everyone cheers me on.*

But in his remarks at a prep-school chapel service in Chattanooga, Wottle set the record straight. He told everyone that his great kick was a myth. "The other runners went out so fast at the beginning that they slowed down at the end; I was able to maintain the same pace that I started with. . . . *Even though it looked like I was kicking on them, they were coming back to me*" (emphasis mine).[2] As one track expert said, "He wasn't kicking, just maintaining in a dying field."

Wottle's example shows us in a powerful way what endurance is: it is maintaining our faithful walk with Christ even when no one else is. In a society of flash-in-the-pan celebrities, trendy spirituality, and well-intentioned Christians, maintaining *is* kicking. Endurance is putting our faith to work by showing up for Christ every day and in every circumstance until the race of life is done.

What does that mean for you? What does it mean to show up for Christ every day in your workplace, in your family, in the challenges you face? Endurance can be expressed in numerous ways. But one specific way is related to the daily annoyances of life—especially in our relationships.

Putting Up with Everyday Annoyances

St. Polycarp, leader of the church in Smyrna, was martyred February 23, 155. The government sentenced him to be nailed to a stake and then burned. They wanted him secured to the stake, of course, so that when the fire raged around him, he wouldn't be able to flee. Polycarp assured them that there was no need for them to nail him to the stake, that he would stand there and die. He asserted that the God who "gives me strength to endure the fire" will also keep me from "moving in the pile."[3]

Polycarp was saying that because he was willing to suffer death, he would be able to stand fast in the pile of burning embers.

This is a classic picture of endurance, of the commitment to suffer anything for the cause of Christ, of the faithfulness that can both stand the fire and stand still, facing anything great or small.

Let me ask you, If our government suddenly outlawed worship, would it stop us from gathering next weekend? I daresay it wouldn't. We would certainly risk a fine or jail time to worship God, wouldn't we? Of course we would. We know that we must be willing to face the fire. I'm confident that most of us would try to be faithful to God.

But here's the conundrum. Why do so many of us who would go to jail to worship God stop coming to worship if the parking lot is too full, or if we don't sing enough of the music we prefer, or if people aren't as nice as we'd like them to be? If we are willing to suffer for Christ, why aren't we willing to be annoyed for him? If we are willing to suffer persecution for Christ, why aren't we willing to suffer irritation?

Interestingly enough, that is what this word *endurance* means here in 2 Peter. It means the commitment of a martyr applied to life's everyday irritations, showing others the same patience that God shows us.

For many of us, this is very difficult. I don't have a Christian bumper sticker on my car, because the way most people drive can cause me to act in very unChristian ways! I may be ready to act like a Christian when someone challenges my faith head-on, but often I'm not when someone cuts me off on the freeway. Endurance is self-control applied to circumstances and relationships. It is about having patience with irritations and with people who absolutely annoy us.

I am not talking about suffering abuse or letting rudeness go unconfronted. I am not saying that to endure is to stay silent, especially when faithfulness demands speaking up. We are not talking about appeasing people or passive-aggressively seething under a facade of spirituality. I am saying we should not let annoying people or irritating circumstances keep us from being faithful to Christ.

I've needed to talk frankly about this with my congregation in San Clemente. As we began a huge campaign to renovate our campus, we acknowledged that even coming to worship was going to be a bit irritating. For over two years, the campus would be torn up, parking would be a headache, some of our favorite programs would have to be postponed, and the dust and noise would be relentless. But we decided as a congregation that one of the best ways we could demonstrate to a watching world that our faith makes a difference would be to endure the changes with patience and good humor, looking to the future. We committed to each other that no matter how difficult it became, we were going to keep showing up for Christ and keep putting up with irritations. And that attitude made a huge difference.

Our consultants warned us that attendance and giving would drop dramatically during construction, but we experienced the opposite. Our attendance grew by nearly 9 percent a year. I think a lot of people in our town were curious not only about the construction but also about the community of faith that endured it so well.

For our faith to make a difference in the real world, we need to show up "for work" every day. The key is to keep going back to the beginning of the passage, to the power of God given to us for life and godliness, to the promises of God we trust with all our hearts. Endurance is possible only with God's help. We may be good some of the time, wise occasionally, and self-controlled often, but to endure over time, we need God at work in us through our faith.

Conclusion: Being a Church of Steves

When I think of people who demonstrate endurance, who show up for Christ every day and put up with others, I think of my friend Steve. Steve is a faithful husband, the father of two girls, an elder in the church, and a real-estate appraiser. He cares for his aging parents, he gives generously to the work of Christ, and he can tell a great joke.

He does nothing that anyone would consider spectacular. He'll never receive a standing ovation, and his hometown will probably never have Steve Day in his honor. But every day, he eats his oatmeal, reads his Bible, does honest work, plays with his daughters, sends email to friends, hugs his wife, and says his prayers before he goes to sleep.

When others left his church during the hard times, he stepped into leadership. When others compromised their ethics to get ahead financially, he stayed true. When colleagues sacrificed family to get promoted, he scaled back, preferring more time with his daughters to having more stuff in his garage.

When others are cynical, Steve is hopeful. When friends are in trouble, Steve is there with a smile, a helping hand, and an open wallet. He is a solid, dependable, caring man whom I can count on for anything, from walking my dog to raising my children if I should die.

One of the things I love about my church is that it is filled with people like Steve. Most of them will never get a standing ovation from a crowd; most people will never even notice what these everyday heroes are doing.

They are simply staying faithful no matter what comes their way. I have looked at them and marveled.

There is the couple who has been married for sixty-five years that now depends on our visitation team so that they can celebrate communion. There is the man in our church who, despite a very active life and career, spends a great deal of his time caring for his wife, who has Alzheimer's disease. There are those who have buried spouses or even their children and still trust in Christ. And there are many who care for both their parents and their children at the same time.

There are leaders who have given countless hours to huge projects, never seeking acclaim. There are small groups of people who faithfully prepare communion, stuff our bulletins, and count our offerings every week. They are unnoticed, but they are irreplaceable, both in God's economy and in our church family's life.

Moreover, members have had to put up with all the irritating things that I, their pastor, do sometimes. As I consider my church's exciting future, I am all the more grateful for all the people who were committed to the church during a stretch of difficult years; their persistence gave us the foundation on which all of our current growth is built.

For these everyday heroes, I wish I could rent a stadium and offer my own standing ovation. I know they didn't do their work for anyone's acclaim, but they are worthy of being honored.

Questions to Consider

1. Think about someone whom you consider an everyday hero. What is it about him or her that warrants your regard?

2. Why does self-control lead to endurance?
3. The word for endurance usually refers to being willing to suffer patiently for our faith. In this passage, it refers to suffering irritations, especially from other people. Which is harder for you? Why? Why do you think that being willing to patiently put up with people is essential to living out a faith that makes a difference in the real world?
4. Is there any area of your life in which you need endurance right now? Ask God to help you be faithful in that situation.

6 REFLECTING WELL

For this very reason, you must make every effort to support your faith with goodness, and goodness with knowledge, and knowledge with self-control, and self-control with endurance, and endurance with godliness.

NRSV

Let this constancy of character reveal integrity of actions and beliefs, both in worship and in life.

author's translation

Giving Religion a Good Name

In this chapter, we will explore one of the least popular words in American culture. Although it is a word that is associated with the church, even Christians avoid using it. The word is *religion*.

Surprisingly, as we'll learn from our next character quality, faith that produces a life commendable to unbelievers includes—no, requires—a religious life. Faith is not enough; individual character is not enough. Faith that makes a difference in the world produces religion that makes a difference in our lives. And religion that makes a difference reflects the very character of God.

Just as I Am

Twenty years ago, I took a group of high school students to a Billy Graham Crusade at the Big A—Anaheim Stadium, which is what Edison Field was called before it was renamed. We walked into the jam-packed stadium, found places high up in the outfield seats, and settled in to hear this legendary preacher. As a young youth evangelist, I wasn't searching for God, but I had brought some teenagers from my Campus Life club who were.

It was a great evening, and Dr. Graham's sermon was a classic. As I listened to his words, I prayed for my young friends. At the end of the message, Dr. Graham gave the invitation. It was probably the same one he had given thousands of times to millions of people all over the world. It was the same one that thousands of other evangelical preachers have used in churches all over the world. It was the same invitation that I myself offered to teenagers virtually every week.

It went something like this: "Jesus said, 'I am the way, the truth, and the life, and no one comes to the Father except through me,' and today, with a simple confession of faith, you can have a personal relationship with God. There is no church to join, nothing to sign, no money to give. It is the free gift of grace to all who will simply confess their need for Jesus to be their personal Lord and Savior. Tonight you can leave here with a personal relationship with Jesus Christ."

I believed those words with all my heart, and I still do today.

As he finished the invitation, the choir began singing "Just as I Am." I remember singing along, the power of the words gripping me again.

Just as I am, without one plea,
but that Thy blood was shed for me.
And that Thou bidd'st me come to Thee,
O Lamb of God, I come, I come.

Just as I am, Thou wilt receive,
wilt welcome, pardon, cleanse, relieve;
because Thy promise, I believe,
O Lamb of God, I come, I come.

As we began to sing, one of my students, Robert, went forward. He became a Christian that night. Afterward, he was full of the joy of knowing Christ, but he felt some apprehension. He, like me, came out of a highly organized and somewhat rote religious background. He was, like I had been, apprehensive about what this step meant for him. So now that he had become a Christian, what did he have to do?

I told him what I told many kids back then. "It's not about being religious; it's about being a Christian. It's not about going to church; it's about following Christ. This isn't about religion; it's about a relationship."

At that time in my life, I was a deeply committed Christian, but I hardly went to church. If you had asked me what I thought I would be doing in twenty years, I would have answered "pastor" no sooner than "flamenco dancer." I wanted everything to do with God; I wanted nothing to do with organized religion.

And while I still believe every word that Dr. Graham said, and while I still invite people to trust and follow Christ personally, I have come to see the problem with my antireligious view of Christianity. It's not biblical.

In our biblical text, we have run right into a religious word. In fact, it shows up twice. And as every would-be exegete learns in seminary, repetition in the Bible is intended to emphasize something to the reader.

The word is *godliness*, and in other verses, such as 1 Timothy 3:16, it is translated as "religion." It refers to the personal and corporate commitments we make as a sign of our devotion to God. We learn from this text that godliness is both our piety and our practice, both our inner spiritual lives and our corporate worship lives. We learn that our faith—if we truly want it to be respected by those in the world—must produce not only character but also consistent acts of devotion.

Now, this may seem strange to us. Why would anyone in the world care about my church life? Why would secular people give a hoot about the way I practice my religion?

Reconsidering Religion

The word *religion* comes from the Latin word that means "to bind" or "to commit," so we could say that godliness means demonstrating our inner devotion to God in acts of binding commitment. It is our worship life, our church life, our ethical life. It is our faith making a difference *in* church.

Because 2 Peter is giving us a list of what we would call secular virtues from Greek culture, a catalog of what the popular culture of the day found commendable, it is interesting that one of those qualities that was considered most commendable is a sincere, devout godliness or religion. I believe that people still find this commendable today.

In Gallup's annual poll of the most respected people in the world, Billy Graham has been named more than any other person in the last fifty years. Pope John Paul II is always mentioned, and until her death, the most admired woman in the world was Mother Teresa. Even in such a potentially antireligious institution as professional sports, Hakeem Olajuwon, a devout Muslim, could be called by *Sports Illustrated* the "most widely respected player among his peers," in part because of his well-known devotion to his religion. Before he retired, he would observe the month-long fast of Ramadan even though it occurs during basketball season.

In other words, even nonreligious people respect and admire those who are devout, sincere, and dedicated to their religion. And that is exactly what this passage refers to. It is telling us that if faith makes a difference, it must produce character that is expressed in consistent devotion to the practices of our faith. The world wants to see if we can "walk our talk." Unbelievers want to see if it is possible for a community of believers to live out their shared commitments. And I believe this is why the biggest stumbling block to unbelievers who are seeking God is not Jesus but Christians, not faith but church.

In his book *Exit Interviews*, William Hendricks reveals the results of interviews with people who have left Christian churches. Their reasons for leaving were various, but a common theme was that when people leave the church, they are not leaving God. They leave because they are deeply disappointed in the people of the church. They came looking for a community of people committed to their convictions, and they leave saying that the church is little different from any other group in the world.[1]

Even people who are exploring the faith are looking to see if what we believe really makes a difference in the way we practice our faith. Is our faith demonstrated in godliness? Do our beliefs produce genuine religion? Or is all this just some kind of social game? The people interviewed told story after story of the difference between what people said they believed and how they acted—even at church.

So the next step in following Jesus into the real world of Monday to Saturday is to consider how well you are doing on Sunday. Genuine godliness results in an authentic church.

So how do we produce this godliness?

The beginning of this passage reads, "His divine power has given us everything needed for life and godliness" (v. 3 NRSV). For faith to be fruitful and effective, with the devout integrity that even unbelievers respect, it must be lived out humbly, publicly, and regularly.

Live Humbly

The word *humble* comes from the word *humus*, which means "earth." To live humbly means to be "down to earth." It doesn't mean having a low opinion of ourselves; it means having an accurate perception of ourselves as mere creatures of earth. To be humble means to understand that first and foremost, we are creatures of the dust whose very lives were given to us by God, that our existence comes from the divine kiss that gave us the "breath of life" (Gen. 2:7).

Notice that our 2 Peter passage about faith that makes a difference does not begin with us or even with our faith. It begins with God. "His divine power has given us everything needed for life and godliness" (NRSV).

The Christian life is a humble life because it begins with the admission of our brokenness and our need for God, and it continues as a life of response to the divine power of God. The church is nothing more than a gathering of people who know that if we are left to ourselves, we'll die. Indeed, we bring nothing to our salvation except the sin that makes it necessary. We acknowledge that without God's gracious intervention, we wouldn't even seek God. We live our lives absolutely dependent on God's divine power. This belief must be at the core of our religious practices. From it, our religious behavior follows; when we forget it, our faith becomes ineffective.

When we forget our humble status, we are tempted to treat church membership like membership in any other social group. It is tempting to think that the more we attend and the more we give, the more benefits we deserve. It is easy to fall into the habit of assuming that the church is here for our convenience, to reflect our preferences, to be a gathering place for our little group of friends. Quickly, without even intending it, we begin to act presumptuously, looking out for ourselves and missing opportunities to extend ourselves in welcome and friendship.

Former Senate chaplain Richard Halverson once said that the church is the only social institution in our society today that exists for the benefit of its nonmembers. We exist not to make ourselves more comfortable but to serve others.

If you and I live each day aware that the only reason we have faith at all is because of God's gracious love and divine power, we will treat each day like a gift and an opportunity to express gratitude to God; we will treat each worship service as a giving back to the God who saved us, each church event or gathering as an opportunity to offer others the same love and power that we have received. If we live humbly, the church will be a group vastly different from any club or organization in which membership is earned, bought, or secured through social connections. It will instead be a true community that with the love and graciousness of

Jesus welcomes all people and slowly forms all people to become more like Jesus—whether at church or in the real world.

Practice Piety Publicly

This book was born of the pain of Christians who have had to "live down" the inconsistent lives of other believers. Undoubtedly, all of us who have tried to invite friends to join us for worship have heard the all-too-common remark that "the church is full of hypocrites," a remark that many times is right on the mark. So much of the hypocrisy of the church results from our tendency to wear two faces: our church face and our real face. Sooner or later, the real face takes over.

God is not just in church or in our religious activities; he is also in our everyday activities—in life, to use the word from the passage. Perhaps, ironically, our Monday through Saturday practices are the key to making our Sunday practices less hypocritical.

Recently I read that almost 40 percent of the people in our country think that clergy are dishonest, manipulative, and fake. Considering the scandals of recent years, this doesn't surprise me, but it also makes me very aware that the most important thing I can do to give credibility to my leadership in the church is to be the same person both when I'm at church and when I'm not. I must be the same person when I'm at the beach, shopping, at a Little League game, or in my neighborhood as I am in my religious practices. This doesn't mean that I preach a sermon while I'm in the sprinkler section of the hardware store, nor does it mean I should be like the Pharisees, whom Jesus criticized for showing off their spirituality. It just means that I have to live out my faith everywhere. Wherever I am,

I must be an authentic, genuine Christian and not just putting on my Sunday best.

For those of us who find it difficult to be publicly Christian, let me suggest two small steps that make a world of difference.

First, be gregarious with gratitude. Whenever possible, express your gratitude to God for all that you have. There is a clear link between receiving grace and being grateful. In a world in which so many want more, to express wonder and genuine thankfulness for what we have softens the skeptics and keeps our hearts malleable to the Spirit. A simple activity to consider, if you don't practice it already, is saying grace at meals, even when you're in a restaurant. This doesn't mean you should pray as loudly as possible while the waitress is stuck holding a hot plate, but expressing gratitude to God for that which sustains us each day will help us be more devout throughout the day.

Second, be quick to confess. So many Christians are convinced that they need to be perfect in order to proclaim their faith publicly. But in truth, it is just the opposite. Everybody knows that no one is perfect. When we are the first to acknowledge our mistakes and take responsibility for our errors, we publicly point to the grace by which we stand (Rom. 5:2). We demonstrate that no matter where we are, we are people who live by and depend on the grace of God and the graciousness that people extend to each other.

To practice public piety is not to wear a religious face but to exercise these two acts of Sunday worship—expressing thanks and confessing faults—every day.

Show Up Regularly

God's power is available to us in our church commitments, in our religion, in our Sunday actions, and as we live publicly. Or as 2 Peter says, in "life and godliness."

In college, I had a writing professor who said that in order to be a good writer, you have to be religious about grammar. He believed that unless you bind yourself to the rules of grammar and practice them every time you write, you will never develop the clear prose and clean syntax that make for effective writing.

What are you most religious about? Some of us are religious about work; some of us are religious about exercise or reading the *Wall Street Journal*. Hopefully all of us are religious about hygiene. Whatever you do regularly, whatever you order your life around, whatever sets the pattern of your life or is your binding practice is your religion.

So let me challenge you to one binding church commitment. Let me encourage you to be religious about this one little rule. Let it order your life and regulate your living: Show up. Show up regularly. Show up religiously.

Once we realize that our religious life is nothing but a humble response to God, we'll understand that God is always, always, always reaching out to us, calling us to him, inviting us to listen to and learn from him. Godliness is nothing more than answering the call by showing up.

I don't mean just showing up to worship, though that is a pretty clear biblical command. And I don't mean showing up with false fronts, fake prayers, and church manners. What I mean is that for faith to make a difference in the real world, we must, as often as possible, show up before God as we really are. We must come before him holding nothing back. Whether we come with doubts and struggles, in public or at church, we should make it a habit to bring our real selves before the real God regularly, in worship, in prayer, and in confession.

People desperately want an authentic spiritual community. They want to be part of a community that is real, humble, and devout. They come to church to be with true believers, those who are genuinely and authentically devout. This is why it is not enough to focus only on our own inner spirituality. For faith to make a difference in a world of people looking for a real encounter with God, the entire church must be different.

In her groundbreaking book, *The Shelter of Each Other*, psychologist Mary Pipher tells of how our "toxic" culture, which is fueled by the media, consumerism, and the breakdown of extended family, has led to widespread and pervasive pain stemming from the kinds of dysfunction we are used to seeing in urban centers. In her work with rural teenagers and families, she attests to an alarmingly similar degree of eating disorders, promiscuity, depression, and suicide among "small town kids" as we expect among kids in large metropolitan areas. Pipher believes that the remedy is not just helping individuals work through painful issues but also restoring a sense of community—even in small towns!—in which we can "shelter each other" through deep relationships, authentic commitment, and a conviction to stand together to challenge the destructive values of our culture.

As a pastor, I believe this is the role of the church. While so often we think of the church as a hospital for broken people, I believe we are also called to be a community of health and wholeness. The church is not primarily an institution but an organism; we are "members one of another" (Rom. 12:5). We offer the world not just right doctrine or life-changing experience but a community grounded in the truth, and we experience genuine transformation by worshiping God together and supporting each other as we live differently in a world that is "corrupted by lust."

The Christian life is not a solo endeavor. What makes the biggest difference in the world are not individual saints but godly communities.

Conclusion: "Just as I Am; Just as We Are"

Imagine what a difference it would make if those of us who have learned to come to Jesus "just as I am" started coming to church "just as I am." Imagine how different would be the quality of our worship, the sincerity of our fellowship, the authenticity of our friendships, the care for our guests if each of us were dedicated to coming before God "just as I am," without fakery, with no desire to impress anyone, just our humble real selves living before God's face, whether at church or in public. Let what we sing about Jesus be true of Jesus' people.

> Just as I am, tho' tossed about
> with many a conflict, many a doubt,
> fightings and fears within, without,
> O Lamb of God, I come, I come.

If godliness is living out a genuine and vibrant faith that results in an authentic and real church, then the simplest life-changing, mind-changing thing we can do is live out our faith humbly, publicly, regularly, and authentically. Just as we are.

Questions to Consider

1. Have you been taught to see religion and a relationship with Jesus as opposing forces? Do you see religion as a good thing? Why or why not?

2. What are you most religious about? A career? A hobby? Are you religious about the right things?
3. What is the most difficult part of being public about your faith? Is it difficult for you to let people know that you are a Christian?
4. This chapter discusses some ways to practice piety publicly, of helping to give Christian religion a good name to unbelievers. What other ways could you practice your piety publicly?

7 Not You or Me but We

For this very reason, you must make every effort to support your faith with goodness, and goodness with knowledge, and knowledge with self-control, and self-control with endurance, and endurance with godliness, and godliness with mutual affection.

NRSV

Let this constancy of character reveal integrity . . . especially in the Community of Faith through loving vulnerability and generous mercy.

author's translation

Leaving the World Behind

Sometimes less is more. Consider this quip from the Internet:

The Declaration of Independence: 1,300 words
The Gettysburg Address: 286 words

The Ten Commandments: 179 words
The Lord's Prayer: 66 words
God so loved the world: 5 words
I forgive you: 3 words
I love you: 3 words
The United States government regulation on the sale
of cabbage: 26,911 words

Now, this may be an urban legend, but it makes the point. Faith that makes a difference is a simple subject, but it's not an easy one. Indeed, as we have seen, faith that develops character and makes our lives effective and fruitful is more rigorous and relational than we may have realized. In this vein we now move even more deliberately from inner qualities of the heart to external habits of living. While we have sought to display character that is admired even by unbelievers in our world, if our faith is to have an impact, we must be prepared to leave the world behind.

In 2003, American cyclist Lance Armstrong won his fifth consecutive Tour de France, tying the record for consecutive victories. This cycling race is the most famous in the world, and Lance has become a national icon not only because he has won it five times but also because he did so after beating cancer.

Just a couple of weeks after his third victory in 2001, *Time* magazine ran an article on how Lance used others' doubts about his health to psych out his most formidable opponent, Jan Ullrich, during the most strenuous climbing stage of the race. For most of the day, Lance stayed behind the German cyclist, and whenever a TV camera focused on his face, he grimaced and panted. Word got out to Ullrich's team that Lance, who is usually the strongest climber in the world, didn't have his usual stamina. So Ullrich kept to the front, and his team pushed the pace.

But then, right as the race hit its most grueling point, Lance rode up even with the German leader, matched him pedal stroke for pedal stroke, stared at him for a moment, and then sprinted up the mountain. Lance had not been exhausted at all; he had simply been drafting behind, reserving his strength, letting Ullrich's team break the wind and make his ride easier. When the right time came, he bolted ahead, never to lose the lead.

As we have systematically covered several character qualities using words that were typical of Greco-Roman virtue lists, we have demonstrated that Christianity leads to character that is at least as virtuous, wise, self-controlled, enduring, and devout as that formed by popular ancient moral philosophy. But now we turn to two qualities that are beyond the scope of classical virtue lists.

Like Lance Armstrong in his race with Jan Ullrich in the mountains of France, so far we have been drafting behind the philosophy of first-century Stoicism. Now we leave behind the virtues of both that culture and ours and charge ahead, demonstrating the true strengths of Christian character, the true power of Christian witness, the winsome, engaging, and inspiring quality of faith expressed as love.

This is a crucial step for our witness to a faith that makes a difference in the world, as well as for our own deeper understanding of what true Christianity is all about.

Comedian Rita Rudner once observed that if you put flour and water together, you have glue. If you add butter and eggs, you have the makings of a cake. Similarly, if you put faith and good works together, you get a self-righteous sticky mess. If you add love, however, you have the makings of a true Christian.

If we stop at a faith that has virtue, wisdom, self-control, endurance, and godliness, we have the sticky mess of half-baked moralism. But with mutual affection and love, we produce a feast of true Christian faith.

Looking Closely at Love

Our final goal is *agape* love, the love that is like God's love, the love with which "God so loved the world, that he gave his only son," the unconditional love of God offered without thought of receiving, offered even to enemies. But we'll discuss that in the next chapter.

Before we can take love out into the world, we have to talk about love in the community of believers, love for our brothers and sisters in Christ, what Francis Schaeffer called "the mark of a Christian."

In John 13:34–35 we read Jesus' words: "Just as I have loved you, you also should love one another. By this everyone will know that you are my disciples, if you have love for one another" (NRSV).

Notice the word "everyone." Jesus told his disciples that their witness to "everyone" depends on how people see them treat each other. The mark to the world that we are Christians is the love we have for each other. The phrase "mutual affection" expresses the same idea. It comes from the word *philadelphia* or "brotherly love." It is not a metaphorical "brother-like love" for all people but a commitment to fellow Christians as actual brothers and sisters.

Interestingly, in the Bible, *philadelphia* or, as it is best translated, "mutual affection" is most often used in reference to equality. It means that while the world may be torn by class, race, and gender divisions, while numbers of people may feel that they are higher than others or may be treated as lower than others, in the fellowship of

Christ, where God is Father, we are all equal as brothers and sisters. As Paul put it in Galatians 3:28, "There is no longer Jew or Greek, there is no longer slave or free, there is no longer male and female; for all of you are one in Christ Jesus" (NRSV).

This thinking was radical in its day. It was countercultural. Women who were treated as property were given positions as apostles, teachers, and leaders in the church (Romans 16). Slaves who could be sold and killed were treated as brothers and sisters in the church (Philem. 10–16). Centuries-old racial divisions were healed by the creation of one new humanity that lived together in the church (Gal. 3:28).

This mutual affection was one of the most compelling features of Christianity. Listen to an excerpt from a letter sent by a man named Aristides to the Roman emperor Hadrian around 125: "They love one another, they never fail to help widows, they save orphans from those who would hurt them. If they have something, they give freely to the man who has nothing. If they see a stranger, they take him home, and are as happy as though he were a real brother. They don't consider themselves brothers in the usual sense, but brothers instead through the Spirit of God."[1]

Here's my point. If we are going to demonstrate faith that is effective and fruitful, it must leave behind even the highest aspirations of non-Christian culture and produce an even more admirable way of living. If our faith is going to make a difference in the world, it must produce a quality of love in the church that the world will see and desperately desire.

Effective faith binds believers in shared radical love. Before we can demonstrate the unconditional love of God to the world, we must experience the brotherly love of Christ within the community of God's people. We must exhibit a kind of love for each other that will make seekers in the world acknowledge that there is no other place on earth where they can find it.

So what does this mutual affection look like? How can we live out this brotherly and sisterly love to each other? Let me suggest two points, drawn from the New Testament's consistent teaching on *philadelphia*: mutual affection is expressed in shared lives and vulnerable fellowship, as well as in shared mercy and generous forgiveness.

Shared Lives, Vulnerable Fellowship

During the most recent war in Iraq, our congregation reached out to the wives and families of marines at Camp Pendleton who had been sent into combat. One of our elders is the principal at the base elementary school, and she helped us give a dinner for the families to show our support. At the dinner, I made a brief presentation offering the families of our church as "family partners" for the marine families. Over thirty-five families accepted the offer.

While we extended ourselves to these military families, the church families found that our lives were equally enriched as we, with the military families, prayed for each other, shared meals and emails, and encouraged each other during the long months of conflict. I could tell many stories about our deep and lasting relationships, but I will tell only one.

During the dinner, one of our church members made friends with Mary, a young African American woman with three children under ten and a five-week-old baby. Her husband had been deployed to Iraq just after they had moved to California from the South. Mary and our church member struck up a conversation, and their families became family partners then and there. The

108

next week, Mary and her family were at church, the only African American family in our predominantly white church.

A few weeks after they came to church, I learned that Mary had never had white friends or been to a predominantly white church before and had been very apprehensive at first. But as she felt the love and warmth of the church family, Mary said, she knew that God had brought her to us, and us to her.

One Sunday morning as I stood up to give the announcements and welcome people to worship, I was told that Mary's husband was home and had come to church. I looked across the sanctuary and saw him holding his baby girl, and I said in front of the whole congregation, "Lieutenant, I know we haven't properly met, but I just want to be the first to say on behalf of your new church family, 'Welcome home.'" The whole sanctuary burst into applause, and a number of people shed tears. We had genuinely come to love this family, and they had made a big impact on our church as well.

Mutual affection is different from the love we will discuss in the next chapter. That *agape* love is love that expects nothing in return. This *philadelphia* love is love that both gives and receives. Both Mary's family and her church family partners learned how to give to and receive from each other, and in their friendship, they modeled a different kind of love to our whole church. *Philadelphia* requires that Christians be genuine partners, giving and receiving.

But for many of us, the most difficult part is not giving but receiving. The dominant philosophical worldview that 2 Peter addresses is Stoicism. The Stoic ideal is self-sufficiency. The Stoics believed that the great aim of living was to be as free and self-sufficient as possible. I daresay that if you scratched very deep on many of us, you would find an awful lot of closeted stoics. We are certainly eager to give, but we are petrified of needing anything from others. We feel humiliated if we need help; we would rather die than be dependent on anyone. We want to take care of ourselves so that we are never a bother or burden to anyone.

While self-sufficiency is certainly admirable, it is not the great end of faith. The goal of Christianity is love, and love can only be given if it is first received. Someone once said that "it is better to give than to receive, and it's a whole lot easier." The problem with self-sufficiency is that it is way too easy; it doesn't transform us enough. We can be self-sufficient without having to release our pride. We can be self-sufficient without having to open our hearts. We can be self-sufficient without having to humble ourselves and trust, and we miss out on God's transforming power.

Pastor Jim Cymbala writes:

> When I was growing up, I thought the greatest Christian must be the person who walks around with shoulders thrown back because of tremendous inner strength and power, quoting Scripture and letting everyone know he has arrived. I have since learned that the most mature believer is the one who is bent over, leaning most heavily on the Lord, and admitting his total inability to do anything without Christ. The greatest Christian is not the one who has *achieved* the most but rather the one who has *received* the most [emphasis mine]. God's grace, love and mercy flow through him abundantly because he walks in total dependence.[2]

We receive the most from God when in mutual affection we lean on each other, when we pray for each other, care for each other, depend on each other. I believe that God is waiting to bless you until you ask him to bless you through another believer. I believe that the love of God, whom we call Father, is poured out to his children through their sisters and brothers. And the only way that you are going to have the love of God to give to people in the world is if you will open yourself to receive it within the church.

One of the lessons I had to learn over and over again in the early days of my ministry was a simple but hard truth: we cannot give what we don't have. As my first pastor and mentor, Lloyd Ogilvie, used to say, "God will do through you only what you allow him to do in you." And most often God works in us through another Christian's ministering to us. At least he does with me. I still remember a particularly low point in ministry when a group of men in the church came around me and prayed for me. I was having doubts about my fitness for the pastorate, and I was beginning to think that some of the baggage from my past was going to make it impossible for me to serve God effectively. As this group of older men placed their hands on me and prayed blessings on me, I could sense the healing of God at work within me. It was like I was being bathed in acceptance and covered with their confidence. Tears flowed down my cheeks, and as they served me the Lord's Supper, the Spirit of God nourished my soul. It is a holy memory for me. But at the time, it was really hard to be so vulnerable.

It may be hard for you too. It might mean you need to say to someone, "I need your help. I need your prayers. I am lonely. I am doubting. I am hurting. I am confused." It might mean humbly reaching out to someone and saying, "Please teach me, and please mentor me. Please help me walk with Christ the way you do."

Let's face it. Most of us have a hard time being vulnerable with anyone, especially our brothers and sisters in Christ. Maybe it is the competition. Maybe it is the fact that we always want to impress those closest to us. We might be vulnerable with parents or those who we perceive are "over" us, but it is hard for many of us even to borrow five dollars from our brother or to share a struggle with a sister. Sibling rivalry permeates the church. But in mutual affection, in shared vulnerability, we discover that there is something wonderful about being bound together as equals. Like climbers who take turns securing each other on belay as we seek the pinnacle, we will reach the heights of character-filled faith only as we share our lives in mutual affection, giving and receiving, caring for each other.

Shared Mercy, Generous Forgiveness

For most of us, the struggle to express mutual affection in vulnerable fellowship is directly related to the ways in which people, even Christians, maybe especially Christians, have failed us.

The most painful stories I hear as a pastor are not of life's tragedies but of the heartrending ache that comes from the disappointment in, the insensitivity of, even the betrayal of a brother or sister in Christ. But the church is to be a whole community of forgiven people. Forgiveness of other Christians is absolutely crucial to our experiencing the love of Christ in our lives.

Jesus was so clear about this point that he *ruined* the beloved Lord's Prayer with an emphasis on forgiveness. You see, long ago, the church edited Jesus' words so that they would fit better in worship. When we say the Lord's Prayer, we end with "forgive us our debts as we forgive our debtors, lead us not into temptation and deliver us from evil" and tack on the stirring finale, "for thine is the Kingdom, power and glory forever! Amen!" But when Jesus taught these words in the Sermon on the Mount, he said, "forgive us our debts as we forgive our debtors, lead us not into temptation and deliver us from evil" and then continued with these words: "For if

112

you forgive others their trespasses, your heavenly Father will also forgive you; but if you do not forgive others, neither will your Father forgive your trespasses" (Matt. 6:14–15 NRSV).

Sheesh. Not exactly a rousing finish. According to Jesus (and this is so important that it is the only part of the prayer that he repeats), we must offer forgiveness to others as generously as we need it ourselves.

One author describes the challenge of forgiveness as the emotional equivalent of "Everest without oxygen, Wimbledon without a racket, La Scala without a score."[3] Forgiveness is a most difficult task. Forgiveness is not excusing, it is not dismissing, it is not understanding. It is giving up resentment and the right to revenge when someone has harmed us. It is letting go of what we have against someone because of the love of God.

Forgiveness is always difficult. But the most difficult hurts to forgive are family failures. On the stairway from faith to love, we may need a giant leap and a helping hand to take this step. But we dare not get stuck here. Without love and forgiveness, our faith is only a sticky moralistic mess.

Conclusion: The Words We Most Want to Hear

A few years ago, a nationwide poll asked, "What word or phrase would you most like to hear uttered to you, sincerely?" Can you guess the first thing people wanted to hear? Not unexpectedly, it was, "I love you." The second was, "You are forgiven." And number three, believe it or not, was, "Supper is ready."[4]

I wrote my Ph.D. dissertation on the life-transforming communion that the church is supposed to be. But those three phrases may be the best description of the church I have ever read.

113

"I love you." You are my brother, you are my sister, because of the love of God.

"I forgive you." No matter what you do, we can always be reconciled, because of the forgiveness of God.

"Supper is ready." Let's break bread together, let's eat together, let's share our lives together. Let's gather around communion tables and dinner tables and share our lives vulnerably, forgive each other generously, join ourselves together in enduring and loving mutual affection.

God is calling us to be people who take his message of love and gracious acceptance into the world. But before we have the right to say it, we must live it. More than anything else, we need to be a community that communicates to each other in both words and actions: "I love you, I forgive you, supper is ready."

Questions to Consider

1. "Mutual affection" or "brotherly love" is the first character quality in the list that is specifically Christian. Why do you think this is so important? Now, read John 13:35 and John 17:21. What are the results of Christians loving each other?
2. "Brotherly love" in this text is meant to be taken not symbolically (brother-like love for everyone) but literally (we are to love fellow believers as brothers and sisters). Therefore, Christians are to consider each other as family. What are the benefits and the disadvantages of this kind of brotherly love?
3. How does considering each other brothers and sisters in Christ lead to more equality both in the church and in the world? (See Matt. 23:9–10.)

4. Why is mutual affection best demonstrated through forgiveness? Read Matthew 6:14. What are the verses called that immediately precede this one? What is the significance of seeing this verse as part of the Lord's Prayer?
5. Is there any Christian whom you need to forgive? What do you think would happen if you did? What do you need in order to do so? Reread 2 Peter 1:3–4. What does God offer us in difficult situations such as trying to forgive? Ask God to give you his power for mutual affection.

THE ONLY THING
8 THAT COUNTS

For this very reason, you must make every effort to support your faith with goodness, and goodness with knowledge, and knowledge with self-control, and self-control with endurance, and endurance with godliness, and godliness with mutual affection, and mutual affection with love.

NRSV

Last, let all that is produced through your faith lavishly and consistently overflow in redemptive love to everyone in your life.

author's translation

From Faith to Love

As we have been considering what it takes to have a faith that garners respect in the eyes of the world, what we began through a mere trust in the divine power and precious promises of God is now brought to culmination in love. As one scholar explains:

> The whole list [of virtues] is given Christian definition by its first and last items—the only terms whose position in the list is significant. Christian faith is the root from which all these virtues must grow, and Christian love is the crowning virtue to which all the others must contribute. *In a list of this kind, the last item has a unique significance. It is not just the most important virtue, but also the virtue which encompasses all the others* [emphasis mine]. Love is the overriding ethical principle from which the other virtues gain their meaning and validity. Thus the author of 2 Peter sees that some of the ethical ideals of pagan society should also be Christian ideals, but only if they are subordinated to and reinterpreted by the Christian ideal of love.[1]

To love is to live out our faith. To love is to reveal the very character of God in the real world. To be fruitful and effective is to love like God. Or as the apostle Paul puts it in Galatians 5:6, "The only thing that counts is faith working through love" (NRSV).

But real love for the real world takes real work.

Hosea's Love

One afternoon a few years ago, I agreed to lead a question and answer time for a class of fifth graders in our church's Youth Club program. It all started innocently enough. I answered two or three questions about how I became a Christian and when I knew I was being called to be a pastor, when one girl asked me, "What is your favorite Bible story?"

Without hesitating (or thinking), I said, "Hosea. Do you know the story of Hosea?"

118

They all shook their heads, so I jumped right in. "Hosea was a prophet of God." I looked at the innocent faces of those eager kids all focused in on Pastor Tod. "And God told Hosea that he should go and marry . . ." Just then my throat squeezed shut, my forehead started to glisten with beads of sweat, and I could hear an elder behind me starting to chuckle. "Uh . . . umm . . . whom God told to marry (gulp) a prostitute."

I quickly tried to move on, but a hand went up. *Uh oh.*

"Pastor Tod, what's a prostitute?"

Now my elder, being the spiritual leader that he is, was laughing out loud.

I said, "Umm . . . that is someone who lets someone else use their body in bad ways."

"You mean for science?"

"You know," I responded, "maybe your parents should tell you this story."

Sometimes the vulgarity and bluntness of the Bible are overwhelming. But the story of Hosea is my favorite story because, in all its unvarnished detail, God used it to show his people what his character is like. No Old Testament story tells us of the love of God so clearly.

God tells Hosea to marry Gomer, a prostitute. So he does, and God says, in effect, "Tell my people that I am like you, Hosea. I will love my people and keep covenant with them even though they have been corrupted and even fail me." We read in the book of Hosea these words to the people of God: "And I will take you for my wife forever; I will take you for my wife in righteousness and in justice, in steadfast love, and in mercy. I will take you for my wife in faithfulness; and you shall know the LORD" (2:19–20 NRSV). So Hosea does his job and tells Israel that God is like him, joining himself to a discarded and adulterous woman.

Then Gomer leaves Hosea and goes back to prostitution. But God tells Hosea to find her and take her back. When Hosea finds Gomer, she is being auctioned like meat to the highest bidder. God tells Hosea to buy her back. "You redeem her life," God says in effect, "and you tell my people that this is what I am like. No matter what you have done, I will love you and stay with you. I will be faithful to you even when you are not faithful to me. I will keep covenant with you, even when you break covenant with me. No matter how far you fall, no matter how deeply you fail, I will come get you. I will save you. I will buy you back. I will redeem you. You are mine and I love you," says the God who, we will learn centuries later, is love.

In this chapter, we will examine the ultimate objective of Christian faith: love. Not just any love. Certainly not the love of MTV or daytime dramas. Not the love of Shakespeare or Emily Dickinson. Love like God loves. The ultimate end of faith is becoming people whose lives reveal the God who is love.

Author Philip Yancey tells of a British conference on comparative religions in which experts from around the world debated what, if any, beliefs are unique to the Christian faith. They began eliminating possibilities. Incarnation? Other religions had versions of gods' appearing in human form. Resurrection? Again, other religions had accounts of a return from death. The debate went on for some time until C. S. Lewis wandered into the room.

"What's the rumpus about?" he asked, and they replied that they were discussing Christianity's unique contribution among world religions.

Lewis responded, "Oh, that's easy. It's grace, the unmerited love of God."

After some discussion, the conferees had to agree. The notion of God's love coming to us free of charge, no strings attached, seems to go against our every instinct. The Buddhist eightfold path, the Hindu doctrine of karma, the Jewish covenant, and the Muslim code of law—each of these offers a way to earn love and approval. But, Yancey concludes, "Only Christianity dares to make God's love unconditional."[2]

We often hear the term *unconditional love* and consider it the hallmark of all love. But let's be clear here: the only unconditional love is God's love, and God's unconditional love is effectual only with our response. The God who is love will not force his love on anyone; he offers it freely and lavishly. But it requires both our acceptance to receive it and our obedience to display it.

God's love, so freely given, is the motivation for God's saving and sanctifying activity in human history. John 3:16, perhaps the most famous verse in all of the Bible, puts it most clearly: "For God so loved the world that he gave his only Son, so that everyone who believes in him may not perish but may have eternal life" (NRSV).

God's love so freely given has a clear purpose: to redeem his rebellious creatures, to forgive his fallen people. God's love restores humanity to wholeness, and our purpose for living and loving must be nothing less than to spread this wholeness to people around us. So here's the point: faith—faith that is nothing more than trusting in the divine power and precious promises of God, faith that makes a difference in the real world—loves.

Or to put it more exactly, faith that is effective and fruitful produces the same redemptive love in and for the world that God reveals in Jesus Christ.

Our whole reason for being and believing is not just to make it to heaven but to display in our lives the love of God that gives us heaven. It is not just to be people of faith but to be people whose faith reveals the redemptive love of God in Jesus Christ so that others will experience that love also.

So how do we become people who love like God loves?

First, Be Loved

In this book, we have learned that we cannot give what we do not have. In order to love like God, we must first let ourselves be loved by God. We must first experience what author Brennan Manning calls the "relentless tenderness of God."

Manning tells the story of Paddy Chaevsky's play *Gideon*. In the play, Gideon is lying awake in his tent late at night, praying. "Oh God, oh God. Are you out there, God?"

And God answers him, "Yes, Gideon."

"Oh God, oh God, please tell me, do you love me, God? Do you love me?"

"I love you, Gideon."

"You do? Oh, that's nice. But tell me, God, why do you love me? Why do you love me, God?"

"Quite frankly, Gideon, I don't know. Sometimes my love is unreasonable."

If you want to love others like God does, I invite you to receive, believe in, and bask in the unreasonable love of God for you.

If you are a follower of Jesus Christ, you are a beloved child of God. There is nothing you need to do to earn that love; you simply need to believe it and live your life responding to it.

If you have never trusted Christ or allowed the love of God to adopt you, then all you need to do is receive it. I urge you to consider today the love of God that is reaching out to you and take it into your life. It will be like stepping into a gondola that will lift you out of the corruption of the world and take you to the summit of virtue. In the words of St. Augustine, "By loving the unlovable, You made me lovable."

Second, Learn Love

We love like God by learning about love from God. Probably all of us remember asking someone in our lives what seems now like the silliest question: how will I know when I am in love? The answer most likely was, "You'll just know." The assumption, of course, is that love, and loving well, is the most natural thing of all. We all know how to love, right? Well, no. If the bookshelves of Barnes & Noble are any indication, most people are looking to learn how to love.

What is so confusing and painful for so many of us is that we have been loved by fallible people. So if we are going to love like God, we must learn to love from God. We must remember that when the Bible in 1 John 4:8 declares that "God is love," it does not say that "love is God." We can't project human love onto God; instead we allow God himself to teach us love.

This is why this passage is so important. In it we find love defined through character. If love is the very crown and summation of all the character qualities in this passage, then to love like God loves requires faith, virtue, wisdom, self-control, endurance, godliness, and mutual affection. It is not the rush of emotion or the fragility of human need; it is instead the full expression of the redemptive affection of God found in Jesus Christ.

The apostle John also writes, in 1 John 3, "We know love by this, that he laid down his life for us—and we ought to lay down our lives for one another. . . . Little children, let us love, not in word or speech, but in truth and action" (vv. 16–18 NRSV). Friends, we will learn to love like this only from God himself.

Third, Focus on God, Not on Love

As we attempt to work out our faith in love, we often may be confused. In a complicated world, it is often difficult to discern what is a loving act. Is it loving to give a handout to a street person who may use it to buy alcohol or drugs? Is it loving to support a colleague whose incompetence may be harming the company? Is it loving to keep your opinions to yourself when you see someone heading down a dangerous moral path?

These are complicated issues with no simple answers. Sometimes in trying to focus on love, we can lose our way. But Jesus reminds us that if we keep our focus on God and on obeying his Word, we will express the most loving action. As Jesus said, "Those who love me will keep my word, and my Father will love them, and we will come to them and make our home with them" (John 14:23 NRSV). If we keep his Word, God will be with us and guide us.

Let us remember that God's law is an expression of his love. The commandments of God are the muscles of the divine embrace. They are what holds us in love when we are in danger of falling. They are what hangs on to us in the dark moments when our steps are uncertain. Let me put this as bluntly as possible. It is never loving to sin. The loving act will never go against the Word of the God who is love.

Friends, let me offer this simple word as we seek to demonstrate the redemptive love of God to a watching world. If we can't see clearly what love demands, keep looking to Jesus' commands. Keep listening to Jesus; keep Jesus' Word. Follow the footsteps of the one who, in love, gave his life for the world, and you will love like him.

What's Weighing You Down?

When I was fifteen years old, three of my friends, Drew, Jeff, and Steve, and I decided to take our first backpacking trip without any adults. Looking back, I am a bit stunned and flattered that my folks let me do it. We were so excited about it. The night before, we loaded our packs and tested them out. After laying all of our equipment out on the floor, we divided everything up so that no one ended up carrying more weight than the others.

Once all the packs were filled, I tried mine on. I remember saying, "Hey, this is light. This is no sweat. I am feeling great." The other guys were talking about how heavy their packs were, but I was almost boasting at how easy I thought this was going to be.

That night, I slept fitfully. I was way too excited, and when I woke, I was a bit concerned that I might be a little low on energy for the long day ahead of us. When we arrived at the trailhead, I remember Drew and Steve helping me lift my pack on. When it settled on my shoulders, it felt really heavy. *Sheesh, this is going to be harder than I thought. I wish I had slept better now.*

The first four miles were straight uphill. The load of the pack really weighed on me. The guys were starting to pull ahead, and they gave me a hard time.

"What's wrong, Tod? We thought you were feeling strong. Is the pack too heavy for you? Do you need some help?"

I didn't admit anything, of course, but just kept laboring up the hill.

Finally, from way up ahead, Jeff called back to me. "Hey, we stopped up here so that you can catch up, okay?"

When I finally got to them, I mumbled some apologies for holding them back and asked them to help me slip off my pack for a brief rest. As they took the pack off, three huge boulders came tumbling out and thudded to the ground. My friends had been so bugged by my boasting that they had decided I needed to carry some extra weight.

You know, reading these pages, chapter by chapter, some of us may feel as if we are beginning to stumble under the weight of it all. But remember this: this passage begins with the assurance that we have God's divine power giving us all we need for life and godliness. Jesus himself said that the burden he rests on our shoulders is light and that he will share it with us. If we are genuinely attempting to live out a faith that makes a difference, then we will not be weighed down but lifted up.

So maybe the burden we are carrying is not the responsibilities of growing character or the demands of love. Maybe we are carrying some things we don't need to be. Some of us have no room for love because we are carrying so many big rocks. What are you carrying? Guilt? Secret sins? Hurt? Unforgiveness? What has been stuffed into your life by someone else? Pain? Resentment? Anger? What have you collected along the way that is making the journey seem impossible? Sins? Fears? False beliefs? What do you need to unload so that God can fill you with his character, his love?

As we attempt to live out our faith in the real world, we should pause frequently to consider these questions:

Do you know the love of God?
Will you learn love from God?
Will you keep your focus on God?

If the answers are yes, then you will love.

Questions to Consider

1. Briefly review the list of character qualities that our faith should produce. Which one has been most difficult for you? Why?
2. Describe the kind of person you find most difficult to love.
3. Review each of the three ways that Peter gave us to become people who love like God. What one central thought for each have you learned anew?
4. Which one of these three ways could be a strategy for you to become more loving, like God? Which of the ways is most natural to you? Which is most difficult?
5. What do you most need God to do in your life in order to produce faith that works in the real world?

9 SUREFOOTED FAITH

For if these things are yours and are increasing among you, they keep you from being ineffective and unfruitful in the knowledge of our Lord Jesus Christ. For anyone who lacks these things is nearsighted and blind, and is forgetful of the cleansing of past sins. Therefore, brothers and sisters, be all the more eager to confirm your call and election, for if you do this, you will never stumble. For in this way, entry into the eternal kingdom of our Lord and Savior Jesus Christ will be richly provided for you.

NRSV

But beware! If you neglect these things, you are walking blindly on the edge of a cliff, forgetting that only God's gracious forgiveness has brought you safely to this place in the journey. Therefore, my brothers and sisters, put your faith to work in the real world and demonstrate that it is indeed genuine. If you do this, you will never stumble as you live as a citizen of God's kingdom now and forever.

author's translation

An Unexpected Twist

Well, we have completed the list. We have made it from faith to love and learned a lot about living as effective Christians in everyday life. So we are done, right? It's just time to start "walking our talk," right?

Not so fast.

God wants us all to be people whose lives are effective and fruitful, who really make a difference for him in the real world. God is not particularly interested in saving people just so they can sit around and wait for him to come again. He wants us to be more than just good people. He wants us to be people whose lives of character proclaim and demonstrate the kingdom of heaven to a searching world. The virtues produced by faith—goodness, knowledge, self-control, endurance, godliness, mutual affection, and love—are to be put to use in real-life situations so that other people will come to the knowledge of Jesus Christ.

But after this passage of 2 Peter crescendos to love, there is no charge, no pep talk, no command to get to work. Instead, there is a warning. A warning to keep from stumbling.

Finding Our Footing

Back in my seminary days, I spent a summer working as a chaplain intern with cancer patients at a hospital in Pomona, California. That summer there were eight seminarian interns, one of whom was Tom. Tom was a caring man with a great sense of humor who loved to play guitar and tell stories. We all knew that Tom would be a really fine pastor someday soon. I really liked him.

Just a few months after our internship ended, I received news that Tom had gotten married and soon would be moving to Arizona, where he was being recommended by a church's search committee for his first call as an associate pastor. I was very happy for him. His life was headed in exactly the direction he had prayed it would. The path before him looked smooth and clear.

So you can imagine my shock when I heard that Tom was dead. He had flown to Arizona to preach his candidating sermon. That evening, he decided to hike up a local mountaintop, and he never came home. Somewhere on the trail, Tom had stumbled and fallen to his death.

An investigation determined that Tom most likely had made it to the top of the mountain, taken in the view of what would soon be his parish, watched the sunset, and then decided to take a different trail back down in the twilight. All the locals knew that the other trail was treacherous. They knew that the only safe way to go down was the same way you went up. But no one told Tom. After making it safely to the pinnacle, he stumbled fatally on the way home.

His grieving bride used her anger and sadness for a good cause. She saw to it that a sign was erected at the top of the mountain warning hikers of the danger of coming down the alternate route.

We who have arrived at the pinnacle of faith have stared at the vista through the eyes of love. But lest all our efforts go for naught, we need to know how to make it safely home.

We can see that the point of this passage is ultimately not just developing character. It is not even just becoming people who live commendable lives before others. Ultimately, faith that works is a continual embodying of what Jesus called the kingdom of heaven. And until we are at home with Christ, we are always in danger of falling. So our writer offers us words of warning. Look closely at the last phrase in verse 10: "For if you do this, you will never stumble" (NRSV).

The word *stumble* here usually means to sin grievously, to commit such a serious moral lapse that our witness to the life-transforming power of Christ is virtually ruined. It is to fall into some temptation that ruins, at least for a time, our ability to proclaim and demonstrate the kingdom of heaven. It's about how our lack of "showing" destroys our ability to do any "telling."

We all know far too many stories of these stumblings. Of moral leaders caught up in public scandal. Of pastors who fall into sexual sin. Of Christians who embezzle money meant for God's work. Of ministries that sully the name of Christ by abusing the trust they are given. Of Christian leaders whose marriages fall apart, or whose children rebel because they have seen too much hypocrisy.

I am willing to bet there is not a person reading this book who hasn't been hindered in their walk with Christ because of the faltering of some Christian walking ahead of them. Falling into sin is not to be taken lightly. It is not okay "because it happens to everybody." It's not something to shrug off. Falling into sin both harms people and mars our witness to the life-transforming power of Jesus. We can't tell people how Jesus is changing our lives if we continually fall back into our old ways.

But let's be very clear here. The church far too often shoots its wounded. We should cease looking with eyes of judgment at those who have stumbled. Many of us shudder when we remember a misstep that could have resulted in our fall. And some of us are still recovering from stumbles and feel very tender.

So if we truly want a faith that works in the real world, we must look at our own sin clearly and call it what it is, we must create a community that tenderly helps up those who have fallen, and we must also dedicate ourselves to learning to walk our entire lives with a "surefooted faith" that increasingly shows the good news of Jesus Christ.

People with surefooted faith are those who day by day in deep dependence and steady obedience continue to follow Jesus Christ as a kingdom person. With each step, the surefooted steer clear of the obstacles that could cause them to ruin their ability to proclaim the difference that Christ makes.

So what does surefooted faith look like? Let me suggest three things. Surefooted faith stands in security, steps toward maturity, and strides through complacency.

Stands in Security

Many of us believe the only way to motivate people to walk without stumbling is to fill them with fear. Oh, fear is an effective motivation in the short run. But ultimately it doesn't inspire surefootedness through the varying terrain of life. Unfortunately, too many churches use the stick of fear far more than the carrot of love.

One of my friends came to me in a crisis and told me that he was contemplating suicide. He had means. He had motivation. It was very scary. I asked him if he had ever felt this way before. He said he had. "The only reason I haven't done it yet is because someone told me that if I commit suicide, I will go to hell."

As I listened to him, I felt sick to my stomach. I weighed my words carefully. I truly felt his life was in the balance. I said, "Listen, I don't want you to take your life. I love you, and I don't want to lose you. But you are a Christian; even if you took your life, you'd be with God in heaven. You don't go to hell for committing suicide. I cannot use the fear of hell to keep you alive. Instead, I want you to choose life out of the security of knowing you are absolutely loved by God."

It was a risky statement, one that was criticized by a mental-health professional when I told her what I had said. But I believe that one of the reasons my friend was suicidal after all those years of living the Christian life was because the fear of hell, and not the security of God's love, had been the motivating factor of his faith. He was so afraid of rejection from both God and people that he was tormented by loneliness, easily slipped into depression, and was unable to sustain healthy long-term relationships. Those issues led him to make some sinful and foolish choices that led to more self-loathing and fear. He needed security to live faithfully.

What does it mean to be "eager to confirm your call and election"? What does it mean that "entry into the eternal kingdom . . . will be richly provided for you"? If we are saved by grace through faith, then how can salvation be provided by our developing character? Isn't this a theological contradiction? Commentators and pastors alike have puzzled over this particular passage. It is even featured in a book on hard sayings in the Bible.[1]

Verse 10 reads, "Brothers and sisters, be all the more eager to confirm your call and election" (NRSV). Notice that it says "confirm," not "earn." To confirm is to ratify by the life you live the salvation that you have received. Even when we talk about stumbling or securing entry into the kingdom in verse 11, we are not talking about gaining or losing salvation. In verse 11, Peter is trying to give us confidence. He is saying that salvation will, in fact, be provided for us by the same God who saved us and lavishly provided for us each character quality that we have learned to put to good use. In his commentary on this passage, John Calvin explains it this way: "God, by ever supplying you abundantly with new graces, will lead you to his own kingdom."[2]

This is further demonstrated by the observation that Peter is clearly addressing *Christians*, whom he calls "brothers and sisters." Peter certainly would not have doubted the eternal salvation of Christ followers. Look at verse 12: "Therefore I intend to keep on reminding you of these things, though you know them already and are established in the truth that has come to you" (NRSV). Peter is not threatening his readers with the loss of salvation; he is reminding them to demonstrate the "truth" of the faith in which they are already "established."

Our motivation for moving forward in faith should not be insecurity or fear but the secure love of Christ, who said, "I will never leave you nor forsake you." The only surefooted motivation for the Christian walk is the love and grace of God in Jesus Christ. We start our journey toward a faith worth talking about by standing in security and then taking steps to grow.

Steps toward Maturity

When reading passages like this, some of us are tempted to believe that the only way to avoid stumbling is to be perfect. So we think, *Well, if I am going to have faith that makes a difference, it must be perfect faith. I must be perfectly good, perfectly knowledgeable, perfectly self-controlled, enduring, godly, affectionate, and loving. The surest way to be surefooted is never to take a false step.* But perfectionism paralyzes us, and we never move forward.

Look at verse 8 again: "For if these things . . . are increasing among you." Notice that the writer tells us that our faith is effective and fruitful as long as it is a faith that is growing. Perfection is not our aim; growth is. And growth involves mistakes, failure, and missteps. Growth requires patience and perseverance.

The "organic" language of this passage (fruitful, increasing) subtly reminds us that growth has periods of dormancy, planting and cultivation, and harvest, bounty, and celebration. To have these qualities ("if these things

135

are yours") and to grow in these qualities ("and are increasing among you") is to demonstrate the reality of a deeply rooted faith which over time bears fruit and flourishes.

Surefooted faith, faith that doesn't stumble into sin, heads into the world wholeheartedly but humbly keeps its head down and its eyes on the goal, steadily increasing in character, vigilant to the very last. Surefooted faith stands in security, steps toward maturity, and finally strides through complacency.

Strides through Complacency

Michael Hammer, who was named by *Business Week* magazine as one of the preeminent management thinkers of the nineties and by *Time* magazine as one of America's twenty-five most influential individuals, was once asked, "What advice would you give to the leader of the twenty-first-century corporation?"

He responded, "If you think you're good, you're dead. The essence of successfully going forward is humility—a recognition that success in the past has no implication for success in the future."[3]

Hammer is saying that the successful in life are those who refuse to rest on their laurels but continue to grow and change. In the same way, the New Testament says that the mature are not people who have fully arrived or who have perfectly mastered every aspect of faith. Mature Christians who make a difference in the lives of others are those who keep going, keep learning, keep producing from their faith the love of God for others.

I don't know about you, but often when my faith is ineffective and unfruitful, it is because I have fallen prey to the coziness of a complacent Christian faith. I come to some comfortable place in my faith and say, *Okay, God, that's enough change, that's enough growth. I am just going to stay here in this cozy spot.* And I ignore the opportunity to express love to someone. I turn away from the person who needs me. I duck the responsibility to demonstrate the difference that Christ is making in my life.

As one person has described it, "Hatred bangs drums. Lust bangs the pulse. Anger bangs the fist. But complacency slides into the soul, unmurmuring, uninvited and unnoticed, with a warm and quilted aura of coziness."[4]

It is so tempting, especially when we have come so far, battled such demons, wrestled against so many temptations, taken steps of faith and trust, stood in obedience, and even made sacrifices to follow Christ. It's as though we have come to a vista, a beautiful serene spot, and want to stay on this peak and enjoy the view.

So we gather with other cozy Christians and sing gratefully of God's amazing grace in our lives: "Through many dangers, toils and snares, I have already come. 'Twas grace that brought me safe thus far . . . now I'll just sit right here." Right?

Wrong.

"'Twas grace that brought me safe thus far, and grace *will lead me home*" (emphasis mine). If our faith is going to work in the real world, then until we are finally home with the Lord, we must move out of our complacency and continue the journey of following Christ and living out the kingdom of heaven.

Conclusion: Don't Fall Off the Page

One of my friends was talking with a group of us about the possibility of his making a major change in his life to fulfill what he believed to be God's call. When we asked why he was willing to sacrifice so much security, to give up such comfort, to take such risks, he said that he had spent the past year studying the Gospels, particularly those places where Christ calls people to follow him. His statement has stayed with me: "People who say yes to Christ and take steps of faith become people who change the world. We even know their names: John, Peter, Andrew, Matthew. But people who don't say yes to following Christ just fall off the page, never to be heard from again."

This was a good reminder and challenge to me. I don't want to be a person who "falls off the page." I want to make a difference in the world for Jesus Christ. I want my life to count.

In the film trilogy *The Lord of the Rings*, Frodo Baggins, a hobbit, meets with the elf queen, Lady Galadriel, in the middle of his quest to take the evil ring to Mount Doom. Galadriel has him look deep into a reflecting pool and shows him a glimpse of the future. She warns him that if he fails in his quest to destroy evil, the consequences will be grave. She tells him that he and the others who are traveling with him will face great temptations to turn to evil instead of finishing the task to defeat it. But she smiles and reassures him, "Even the smallest person can change the course of the future."

With all my heart, I don't want to be a person who falls into sin or settles into complacency. I want to be just one small creature who follows Christ in proclaiming and demonstrating the kingdom of heaven to a world in great need. I believe that Christ is raising up people to receive the gift of divine power that rescues us from the corruption of the world, transforms our character, and produces the kind of fruitful and effective faith that will change our churches, our communities, and our world. All we need to do is keep following, keep growing, keep producing the kind of life that speaks to others effectively about the faith we hold.

"If these things are yours and are increasing among you," you will not stumble. But what if we do stumble? That is the subject of our final chapter and a lesson that Peter is more than qualified to teach us.

Questions to Consider

1. In this chapter, we see the ultimate goal of Christian faith: to live in and embody the kingdom of God as an alternative way of living that is available to all people. How do you understand the kingdom of God? What does it mean for you to live in the kingdom of God here and now?

2. In many ways, this passage in 2 Peter is about giving assurance to believers who are struggling to live out their faith. Why is it important for believers to be assured that we are secure in Christ? Are you more effective and fruitful as a person when you are secure, or when you are insecure?

3. If this passage offers us security about our salvation in Christ, then what do you think it means to stumble?

4. In this final section, we see that the journey of living out a faith that makes a difference takes the narrow path between security and complacency and between growth and perfection. What are potential stumbling places for you on this narrow path? Do you tend to get more complacent, or overly perfectionistic? What do you need in order to be both secure and growing?

5. With every lesson, we return to the beginning of the passage (vv. 3–4). Why is it important to continually direct our attention to the "divine power" and "precious promises" of God? How does focusing on these sources of our salvation keep us living out a faith that works? What do you need from God today in order to keep walking in faith and growing in your ability to embody the kingdom of God?

WHEN SAINTS
10 STUMBLE

A young man in college had just made a life-altering decision. He had decided to change his major and was preparing to tell his parents that he wouldn't be pursuing a career in journalism but instead felt a call to serve Christ in full-time ministry. It was a huge step, but one he took without reservation. All he wanted was to be a minister and to witness to Jesus Christ.

Shortly after making this decision, he was out on a Friday evening with a date. They were on their way to a movie and he needed to make a quick stop at an ATM for some extra cash. As his friend sat in the car, he stood in line to withdraw some money from a bank at a busy urban intersection.

Out of the corner of his eye, he saw a homeless man shuffle by. The homeless man eyed the line of people and cried out in a loud voice, "Does anybody here believe in God?"

While all the others ignored what was clearly a panhandling ploy, the young man looked up at the homeless man, who looked so worn down by the world, and he began to say something, but the words stuck in his throat. The homeless man held his gaze and said, "Well, do you believe in God?" The young man heard someone behind him snicker. He could feel everyone's eyes on him now. He panicked. He felt trapped and embarrassed and unable to speak. He shook his head no and looked away. The homeless man threw up his hands. "It figures," he said. And then he was gone.

If there had been a cock nearby that night in the San Fernando Valley in front of the Bank of America, I am sure it would have crowed, because just days after I had decided that God had called me to the ministry, I denied Christ. I looked into the eyes of a man who asked me a question and, because of my fear of him, because of the snickering strangers behind me, and maybe because I was afraid he would ask me for a few bucks, I said that I didn't believe in God.

When I returned to my car and told my friend what had happened, she listened quietly and then said, "Well, now you know a little of what Peter felt." She was right. Throughout my life and ministry, when I have taken missteps or have failed to live out my faith publicly, I have taken solace in and encouragement from the chief apostle.

Following and Failing Christ

Most of us probably know the story by heart, but it is worth retelling. When Jesus gathered his disciples in the Upper Room for their last supper together, he predicted that one of them would betray him. They all looked around protesting and proclaiming their devotion to Jesus, but none did so more forcefully than Peter. "Even if all the others betrayed you, I would not," Peter said, declaring his readiness to go to prison and to death following Jesus. But Jesus gently set him straight, predicting that even before the night was over, Peter would deny Jesus three times.

And of course, he did. By the time a little girl asked him if he was a follower of Jesus, Peter was so adamant in his denials that he blew up in a profanity-laced tirade. Big bold Peter folded like a cheap deck chair.

When we look back at the conversation between Peter and Jesus in the Upper Room, however, we find an interesting statement. Calling Peter by his given name, Jesus says, "'Simon, Simon, listen! Satan has demanded to sift all of you like wheat, but I have prayed for you that your own faith may not fail; and you, when once you have turned back, strengthen your brothers.' And he said to him, 'Lord, I am ready to go with you to prison and to death!' Jesus said, 'I tell you, Peter, the cock will not crow this day, until you have denied three times that you know me'" (Luke 22:31–34 NRSV).

Early in my Christian life, this text from Luke was a source of great confusion for me. Jesus predicts not only his own death but also Peter's denials. Then Jesus says, "Satan has demanded to sift all of you like wheat, but I have prayed for you."

Notice what he does not say.

He does not say, "I have prayed for you so that you won't have to go through this ordeal." Or, "I have prayed for you so that you will stand firm and die with me." Or, "I have prayed for you so that you won't deny me."

Jesus says none of this. Instead, he says, "I have prayed for you that your own faith may not fail." He then says, "Once you have turned back" (or as another version says, "once you recover"), "strengthen your brothers."

Jesus knows Peter better than Peter knows himself. Jesus knows the future and predicts it accurately. He understands and loves Peter, all the while knowing that he will deny him. And Jesus prays that Peter would be of help to the others because of the failure that he is about to experience.

And we too must learn to express our faith even through our failures. I don't believe that the seeking world is looking for people who are perfect. But they do want to see the difference that following Jesus makes. Three years of eating, drinking, ministering, walking, learning, and living with Jesus did not make Peter into a spiritual giant who understood every mystery and lived with unwavering obedience. Not at all. But it did make one huge difference. Peter, though he failed, knew what to do with his failure.

Two Betrayers, Two Responses

Of course, Peter wasn't the only one to deny Jesus. Judas Iscariot is the famous betrayer of Jesus, the one who received thirty pieces of silver to turn Jesus over to the Roman and Jewish authorities. And most of us probably think that Judas's betrayal was far worse. Peter may have denied Jesus to avoid death, but he didn't betray Jesus and cause his death.

But let's think about that again. Jesus had spent a considerable amount of time with Peter. Peter was the one who knew that Jesus was the Messiah. Peter was one of the disciples who went to the Garden when Jesus prayed for help. Peter was the one on whom Christ had promised to build his church. And Peter was one of the inner three, one of Jesus' best friends. In many ways, Peter's denial is even more unthinkable than Judas's.

So what's the difference? Why is Peter honored today, while Judas is still considered a traitor? It's not because of the gravity of their failures. It is because of what they did with their failures.

Both Judas and Peter had walked three years down the same road, but Judas still had not learned to trust Jesus. Judas wanted to take things into his own hands. He betrayed Jesus, and then in remorse, realizing he'd been a pawn for Jesus' enemies, he took his failure into his own hands and killed himself.

This is where Peter was truly a different person. Peter had learned to trust Jesus, especially with his failures. Ultimately, he took Jesus at his word.

Jesus' Prayer for Stumbling Saints

I often imagine Peter wandering through Jerusalem that terrible morning of the crucifixion, staying at a safe distance but hearing the crowd call for Barabbas. I imagine him watching in horror as Jesus is whipped and beaten, as a cross is thrown on him and the executioners lead him off to the hill they called the Skull. It must have felt like a knife turning in his gut to see his Lord, the one he had pledged to follow in life and in death, take the steps alone.

Did the words ring in his ears? "Simon, Simon, listen! Satan has demanded to sift all of you like wheat, but I have prayed for you that your own faith may not fail."

"I have prayed for you that your own faith may not fail." That was Jesus' emphasis. In your failure, don't let your faith fail. Don't let this misstep lead you to abandon the journey. Don't let this spiritual collapse stop your spiritual journey.

As a pastor, I know too many people who have simply stopped following Jesus. Some have abandoned the faith after believing that they just can't measure up. Others still believe, but they now try to survive the challenges of the world by keeping their heads down and their mouths shut. They haven't given up on the faith; they have just given up on the hope that *their* faith can make a difference to other people.

Jesus built his whole strategy for changing the world on this disciple who cowered in front of a little girl. Jesus knew that Peter would fail his first test as a public witness. And as he prepared for his own death, Jesus prayed for Peter. I believe he was praying both for Peter's faith and for the confidence that Peter would need to get back up, dust himself off, and join the fight again. Because for faith to make a difference, we must keep putting it out there. We must not let our failures stop us from doing good. For our faith not to fail, we must trust that Jesus can use our failures for good.

Using Failure for Good

Jesus prayed that Peter's faith would not fail, but he also added a charge: "And you, when once you have turned back, strengthen your brothers." Jesus doesn't just tell Peter to hang in there and hang on. He instead challenges Peter to use even the coming failure for the good work of being a witness for Christ and an encouragement to other stumbling followers.

He does not say, "Once you have turned back, get some comfort from the other disciples." He says just the opposite: "Once you come back, use your personal failure to strengthen your brothers and sisters, your friends and companions. Build on this and let the rest of the community learn from this hard lesson."

For some people, this is the greatest leap of faith. As you have been trying to learn how to live out the list of virtues, a nagging voice has been telling you that because of some failure, you are doomed to an inconsequential Christian existence. You may think that you have been disqualified from ever being able to say anything publicly about your love for God and your faith in Christ. You believe that your witness is ruined.

Let me ask you, Can you believe that Jesus wants to use even your failures for his glory? Can you? Because that is what Jesus wants you to believe.

With every misstep, you have the opportunity to strengthen others by humbly pointing to the only one who is really faithful, virtuous, wise, and self-controlled. With every stumble, you can let others know that you live in daily dependence on the one who can endure anything, who is genuinely godly, who is tender in affection, and demonstrates to the world the unconditional, unwavering love of God. And with every hard-knock lesson, he wants you to grow a bit more into a person who, eventually, won't fail him.

From Stumbling to Striving

Christian history is filled with stories of how God transformed people from sinners who rebelled against God into believers who lived for him. Before he was the apostle to the Gentiles and the writer of most of the New Testament, Paul was a religious fanatic who persecuted the church. Before he was the greatest theologian in Christian history, St. Augustine was a playboy professor who sired a child out of wedlock. Before he was a "fool for Christ" living a life of charitable service that inspired a whole order, St. Francis was a rich spoiled brat. Before he penned his most famous hymn, "Amazing Grace," John Newton was a slave trader. Before he became the greatest twentieth-century apologist, C. S. Lewis was a cynical atheist.

We love to tell these stories. The darkness of a life without Christ makes the postconversion witness for Christ shine all the more brightly.

These are great stories, but we must be careful to avoid implying that once a person has come to faith, faith-filled acts of character and love will follow immediately and without fail. Peter's life and the lessons from the second letter of Peter are more realistic about the process of becoming a person whose life and words speak to a searching world.

Producing from our faith virtues that even a non-Christian would respect does not happen overnight. Effective faith takes time to develop. The basics of the faith must be learned well from good teachers. The character of Christ must be cultivated in good churches. But even more than that, a true witness for Christ comes as we grow through our failures.

Friends, this is perhaps the most important lesson for living out effective faith. For with every failure, we are cast back upon the divine promises of God. With every denial or defeat, we return to square one to learn to produce a genuine, stronger, more vibrant faith. With every sin, we confess our need for grace and mercy as well as our need to be shaped by God's Spirit and transformed more and more from the inside out.

When all is said and done, few people since Jesus had a more effective and fruitful faith than Peter did. But he sure didn't start out that way. Peter denied Jesus because he feared for his life. I denied Jesus because I feared being embarrassed in front of people I didn't know. But what I learned that night was that our failing is never the final word. Even our hypocrisy and weakness can be used by Christ to form us into stronger Christians if we come to him with those failures. To fully follow Jesus, we must trust him with everything, even our failures.

Questions to Consider

1. Have you ever had a cock-crowing moment, a time when you realized you had denied Christ through your words or actions? What impact did that experience have on your life?
2. How did Peter's experience of failing Jesus influence his ministry throughout his life?
3. How should the church change to help people deal with their failures and to avoid them in the first place?
4. In what ways has God used your spiritual failures to strengthen others' faith?
5. In what area of failure or struggle in your life do you need Jesus to meet you? Is there a pastor or Christian friend who could pray with you about this struggle?

EPILOGUE:
A SERMON WALKING

One act of obedience is worth a hundred sermons.

Dietrich Bonhoeffer

Show, *Then* Tell

Albert Schweitzer (b. 1875) graduated college at the age of twenty, became a minister, and earned a Ph.D. from the University of Strasbourg. He became both an accomplished theologian and an equally respected classically trained organist and the leading authority of his day on Johann Sebastian Bach. At age thirty, he went back to medical school and became a doctor, and in 1913, he and his wife, who was a nurse, left Europe for Africa, where they established a missionary hospital for patients with leprosy. They served in Africa for fifty years. In 1952, he was awarded the Nobel Peace Prize.

According to one story about him, when Schweitzer visited America in 1953, he was greeted in Chicago by a

151

crowd of city officials and reporters. As this bushy-haired, mustachioed, six-foot, four-inch-tall man came off the train, the reporters and officials crowded around him with cameras flashing and heaping praise on him.

Schweitzer politely thanked them, but looking over their heads, he spied something that caused him to ask the officials if they would excuse him for a moment. He quickly walked through the crowd until he reached the side of an elderly African American woman who was struggling with two large suitcases. He picked up the bags, escorted the woman to a bus, smiled, and wished her a safe journey. As he returned to the officials, he apologized for keeping them waiting. One member of the reception committee said to another, "That's the first time I ever saw a sermon walking."

Show and Tell: Earning the Right to Be Heard

What Schweitzer could inspire through a simple wordless act is the goal for every believer who wants their faith to make a difference in the real world: to earn the respect of unbelievers by the way we live so we can share with them what we believe. Of course, this is not a new idea. As a young youth evangelist, I was taught that we were to earn the right to be heard. And that is ultimately what we are trying to do when we go into the world to "show and tell" the gospel of Jesus Christ. We are demonstrating and proclaiming that we have been saved by God's power, whisked by faith to the summit of a relationship with the living God, and then patiently tutored in how to live out that faith as a walking sermon:

- as people of genuine godly virtue, applying that goodness with wisdom in real-world situations.

- as people who can demonstrate to a pleasure-satiated world that true pleasure, true happiness, is found in living within the boundaries of self-control.
- as people who maintain and endure to the very end in a world in which everything is disposable and the half-life of any value or commitment is as short as the next news cycle.
- as people who walk their talk about their faith, with religious commitments that are genuine and worthy of respect; free from the hypocrisy and hurt of a nominal Christianity but full of the devotion that makes the world know we mean what we believe.
- as people who have a deep affection for their fellow travelers on the journey of faith. In a world of facades and stoic individualism, we live as those who are authentic and vulnerable with each other, lavishly forgiving each other's faults and embracing each other when we fall.

All of this to the end that we show the unconditional, redemptive love God lavished on us in Jesus Christ before we tell about it. We are trying to "preach the gospel at all times" so that we can speak the gospel with words too.

Make no mistake. We are called as followers of Christ to share the Good News of Jesus Christ so that all people will experience the eternal life that God offers them. We know that as followers of Jesus Christ, we are commanded to go into all the world and proclaim the Good News (Mark 16:15), to make disciples of all peoples (Matt. 28:19–20), to be witnesses to Jesus Christ (Acts 1:8), and to provide a gentle defense of the hope that is within us (1 Peter 3:15–16). We are indeed called to do some telling.

But let's begin with showing. Let us all commit to be, like Schweitzer, a "sermon walking." Personally, I have always been inspired by that description. Even more than I want my sermons to reveal God when I speak on Sunday, I want my life to reveal God on Monday through Saturday. I want the people closest to me to say that I lived out what I believed. And I believe that is what you want also.

As for me, I want my children to know how God loves them by the way that I love them. I want them to know how Jesus calls them to live by watching the way I live. I want my neighbors and friends and family to glimpse God's character in my character. I want my wife to be able to say that my actions at home are consistent with my words at church. Like every sermon I preach, there will be times when my life will be imperfect and even flawed, but with the support of my fellow Christians and the inner work of God's Spirit, I will strive to be a man whose life speaks to the Christianity I confess.

That's what it means to have faith that makes a difference. That's what it means to show and tell the Good News of Jesus.

NOTES

Chapter 1: Faith That Works

1. Craig A. Evans and Stanley E. Porter, *Dictionary of New Testament Background* (Downers Grove, IL: InterVarsity, 2000).

2. And twenty-three vice lists appear in the New Testament as well, all but two of which also occur in epistles: Matthew 15:19; Mark 7:21–22; Romans 1:29–31; 13:13; 1 Corinthians 5:10–11; 6:9–10; 2 Corinthians 6:9–10; 12:20–21; Galatians 5:19–21; Ephesians 4:31; 5:3–5; Colossians 3:5, 8; 1 Timothy 1:9–10; 2 Timothy 3:2–5; Titus 3:3; James 3:15; 1 Peter 2:1; 4:3, 15; Revelation 9:21; 21:8; 22:15.

3. *Ignatius' Letter to Ephesians*, trans. J. B. Lightfoot, http://www.early christianwritings.com/text/ignatius-ephesians-lightfoot.html.

4. Stats from adherents.com, http://www.adherents.com/adhloc/Wh_52.html#110.

5. Leland Ryken, James C. Wilhoit, and Tremper Longman III, eds., *Dictionary of Biblical Imagery* (Downers Grove, IL: InterVarsity, 2000), 857.

6. Colin Brown, Fuller Theological Seminary.

7. Norman MacLean, *A River Runs Through It and Other Stories* (Chicago: University of Chicago Press, 1979), 4.

Chapter 2: For Goodness' Sake

1. Garrison Keillor, *Vanity Fair*, July 1994, quoted on Homiletics Online, www.homileticsonline.com/subscriber/illustration.

2. D. Martin Lloyd-Jones, "Review of G. C. Berkouwer's *Faith and Sanctification*," *Evangelical Quarterly* 25 (April 1953): 107.

3. George Gallup Jr. and Jim Castelli, *People's Religion: America's Faith in the 90's* (New York: Macmillan, 1989), 21.

4. For two such studies, see *Barna Research Group Report*, December 21, 1999, and October 22, 2002.

5. C. S. Lewis, *Mere Christianity* (New York: Macmillan, 1943), 77.

6. James Luther Mays, ed., *Harper's Bible Commentary* (New York: Harper & Row, 1988), on *Logos Bible Software*, CD-ROM (Bellingham, WA: Logos Research Systems, 2001).

7. D. A. Carson et al., *The New Bible Commentary* (Downers Grove, IL: InterVarsity, 1994), on *Logos Bible Software*, CD-ROM (Bellingham, WA: Logos Research Systems, 2001).

Chapter 3: It's Not What You Know

1. Gleaves Whitney, "The Roots of American Disorder," *Vital Speeches* LXII (October 15, 1996): 17.

2. Richard J. Bauckham, *Jude, 2 Peter*, vol. 50 of *Word Biblical Commentary*, electronic edition (Dallas: Word, 1998).

Chapter 4: To Be a Mighty River

1. David G. Myers, *The Pursuit of Happiness* (New York: Harper Collins, 1992), 207.

2. John Calvin, *Institutes of the Christian Religion*, ed. J. T. McNeil, trans. F. L. Battles, Library of Christian Classics (Philadelphia: Westminster, 1960), 1.1.1.

Chapter 5: Being an Everyday Hero

1. Eugene H. Peterson, *A Long Obedience in the Same Direction* (Downers Grove, IL: InterVarsity Press, 2000), 16.

2. Dave Wottle, quoted by Jay Zuckerman, "In the Face of International Tensions, Wottle Struck Gold," The McCallie School, http://www.mccallie.org/tornadoX/sports/Issue4/davewottle11-15.htm.

3. The exact quote is, "Leave me as I am, for He that giveth me strength to endure the fire, will also enable me, without your securing me by nails, to remain without moving in the pile." *Encyclical Epistle of the Church at Smyrnam: Concerning the Martyrdom of Holy Polycarp*, chapter XIII, http://www.ccel.org/fathers2/ANF-01/anf01-13.htm#P911_166347.

Chapter 6: Reflecting Well

1. William Hendricks, *Exit Interviews* (Chicago: Moody, 1993), 250.

Chapter 7: Not You or Me but We

1. Cited in Charles Colson, *Presenting Belief in an Age of Unbelief* (Wheaton, IL: Victor, 1986), 35–36.

2. Jim Cymbala, *Fresh Faith* (Grand Rapids: Zondervan, 1993), 45.

3. Stephanie Dowrick, "The Art of Letting Go," *Utne Reader*, March–April 1999, 46–47.

4. James A. Harnish, sermon, *Walking with Jesus: Forgiveness*, Tampa, March 22, 1998.

Chapter 8: The Only Thing That Counts

1. Bauckman, *Jude, 2 Peter*.

2. Philip Yancey, *What's So Amazing about Grace?* (Grand Rapids: Zondervan, 1997), 45.

Chapter 9: Surefooted Faith

1. Walter C. Kaiser et. al., *Hard Sayings of the Bible* (Downers Grove, IL: InterVarsity, 1997), 724–26.

2. John Calvin, *Calvin's Commentaries: 2 Peter: Commentaries on the Catholic Epistles*, electronic edition (Albany, OR: Ages Software, 1998).

3. Cited in Rowan Gibson, ed., *Rethinking the Future* (London: Nicholas Brealey, 1997), 104.

4. George William Rutler, *The Seven Ages of Man* (San Francisco: Ignatius, 1991), 94.

Tod Bolsinger (M.Div., Ph.D., Fuller Theological Seminary) is the senior pastor at San Clemente Presbyterian Church in San Clemente, California, and an adjunct assistant professor at Fuller Theological Seminary. He is also the author of *It Takes a Church to Raise a Christian: How the Community of God Transforms Lives*. For ten years, he served on the staff at First Presbyterian Church of Hollywood. He is married and has two children.

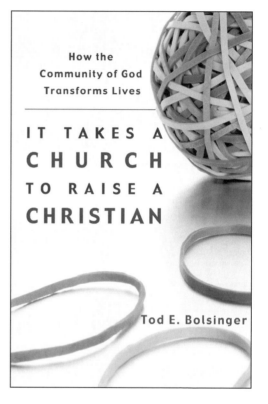